5 MINUTE Church Historian

MAXIMUM TRUTH
IN MINIMUM TIME

DR. RICK CORNISH

NAVPRESS®

BRINGING TRUTH TO LIFE

OUR GUARANTEE TO YOU

We believe so strongly in the message of our books that we are making this quality guarantee to you. If for any reason you are disappointed with the content of this book, return the title page to us with your name and address and we will refund to you the list price of the book. To help us serve you better, please briefly describe why you were disappointed. Mail your refund request to: NavPress, P.O. Box 35002, Colorado Springs, CO 80935.

The Navigators is an international Christian organization. Our mission is to reach, disciple, and equip people to know Christ and to make Him known through successive generations. We envision multitudes of diverse people in the United States and every other nation who have a passionate love for Christ, live a lifestyle of sharing Christ's love, and multiply spiritual laborers among those without Christ.

NavPress is the publishing ministry of The Navigators. NavPress publications help believers learn biblical truth and apply what they learn to their lives and ministries. Our mission is to stimulate spiritual formation among our readers.

ISBN 1-57683-506-5

Cover design by Arvid Wallen

Creative Team: Don Simpson, Eric Stanford, Darla Hightower, Amy Spencer,
        Arvid Wallen, Glynese Northam

Unless otherwise identified, all Scripture quotations in this publication are taken from the HOLY BIBLE: NEW INTERNATIONAL VERSION® (NIV®). Copyright © 1973, 1978, 1984 by International Bible Society. Used by permission of Zondervan Publishing House. All rights reserved. Other versions used include: the *King James Version* (KJV).

Cornish, Rick, 1950-
  5 minute church historian : maximum truth in minimum time / Rick Cornish.
     p. cm.
  Includes bibliographical references and index.
  ISBN 1-57683-506-5
  1. Church history.   I. Title. II. Title: Five minute church historian.
BR145.3.C67 2005
270--dc22

                                              2005015792

Printed in Canada
1 2 3 4 5 6 7 8 9 10 / 10 09 08 07 06 05

FOR A FREE CATALOG OF
NAVPRESS BOOKS & BIBLE STUDIES,
CALL 1-800-366-7788 (USA)
OR 1-800-839-4769 (CANADA)

"This is a great format for our fast-paced society. Rick offers a concise and practical introduction to one hundred of the most significant people and events of church history. Definitely recommended!"

—HANK PHARIS, DMIN
pastor, Calvary Baptist Church, Fargo, North Dakota

"Succinct introductions to major persons and events in church history, replete with suggested applications. Whets the appetite for further study."

—WILLIAM TRAVIS
emeritus professor of church history,
Bethel Seminary, St. Paul, Minnesota

"An easy-to-read, user-accessible guide through the centuries of church history that focuses on people and events. A highly commendable tool for anyone desiring a taste of our Christian past."

—JOHN D. HANNAH, THD, PHD
professor; author of *Our Legacy:
A History of Christian Doctrine*

"The history of the Christian church provides a vivid illustration of God's ability to use fallen human beings to advance His work of redemption and salvation—a revelation beyond Revelations. I hope Rick Cornish's enjoyable sampler of church history will inspire a revival of interest in church history by those of us 'in the pews.'"

—BRYAN DOWD
professor, University of Minnesota

"A short video clip is no match for a feature film, but a good clip hints at the story beyond its boundaries and whets the viewer's appetite to see the film. In this book, Cornish provides one hundred such clips. Each is a story of its own, clearly written and complete with lessons contemporary Christians can learn. But most of all, these clips motivate the reader to go watch the film in its entirety—to learn more fully the magnificent story of Christian history, which is our heritage."

—DONALD FAIRBAIRN, PHD
professor; author of *Grace and Christology in the Early Church*

"This little book is for those who dare to raise unsettling questions about the narrowly individualized and privatized faith that paralyzes the evangelical church today. *5 Minute Church Historian* might be the biggest little book you read in a long time."

—VERNON J. STEINER, PHD
president, The MIQRA Institute

To the Christian martyrs throughout church history (including today) and to my students around the world, some of whom may become martyrs.

The world was not worthy of them. . . .
These were all commended for their faith,
yet none of them received what had been promised.
God had planned something better for us so that only
together with us would they be made perfect.
(HEBREWS 11:38-40)

Contents

PART 9: THE TWENTIETH CENTURY
THROUGH WORLD WAR II (1900–1945)

PART 10: SINCE WORLD WAR II (1946–PRESENT)

Foreword

Some might say that Rick Cornish has undertaken the impossible in this project. And, if Christian history is a warehouse of facts, they might have a point. But Christian history is, as Cornish shows, no warehouse. It is a story. Many facts are here, but there is also a story. Cornish calls it "a spiritual legacy" because he believes that the Christian church is the family of God, and he undertook this "impossible" task to tell the story. I am particularly impressed by the way he is able to relate the details and facts of so many individuals and topics to the continuing living story. This is powerfully important if we are to have a story rather than a warehouse of facts.

G. K. Chesterton once said in his classic, titled *Orthodoxy*, that he always "felt life first as a story" and "if there is a story there is a story teller." Rick Cornish knows that he is not the storyteller. He is simply passing on to others the story as he has heard it.

BRUCE L. SHELLEY
senior professor of church history
Denver Seminary, Denver, Colorado;
author of *Church History in Plain Language* and
Transformed by Love: The Vernon Grounds Story

Acknowledgments

As is true of all three books in this series, many people made *5 Minute Church Historian* possible. My wife, Tracy, and my sons, Scott and Ben, listened to me read these essays and gave up time with husband and father so that I could pursue this project. Eric Stanford, Rachelle Gardner, Don Simpson, Darla Hightower, Glynese Northam, and Nicci Jordan of NavPress guided the book through the writing, editing, and publication processes.

Rhonda Morris, my former office administrator, read the manuscript, finding errors and suggesting improvements throughout. The youth group and parents of Fellowship Bible Church in Tulsa, Oklahoma, tested sample chapters for their suitability for teen readers. Special thanks to my friend Dr. Hank Pharis, who stimulated my love of church history, and Dr. Don Fairbairn, who found and corrected several historical inaccuracies.

This book is partially the result of encouragement from Dr. Bruce Demarest, Dr. Ken Gangel, Dr. Craig Blomberg, Dr. Gordon Lewis, Dr. Bob Osburn, and from NFL Hall of Famer and former U.S. Congressman

Steve Largent. The first to urge me to write this book were Janice David and Joe Seelig. Thanks also to Dr. Bruce Shelley, who generously took time to write the foreword.

Introduction

A typical Christian might summarize church history like this: "When Paul died, the gospel was lost and the church went to pieces. After a long time, Martin Luther showed up and rescued the church. Later, lots of missionaries were sent out. In 1953, my alcoholic grandpa was saved from booze. Since then, my family members have all been Christians, and here I am." Most of those statements contain some truth (assuming this Christian accurately dated Grandpa's conversion), but surely a few more events happened along the course of church history.

Another version sounds like this: "When I was in college, a guy in the dorm told me about the Four Spiritual Laws, and I believed in Jesus. But I'm not into history, so I haven't read much. Jesus died for me two thousand years ago; now I'm going to heaven when I die. What happened between His death and my salvation doesn't really matter."

Those renditions of church history are not complete fabrications; I've heard variations on each more than once. But isn't there more to church history than Paul, Martin Luther, one's own family, and oneself? And doesn't it matter today, at least a little? I propose that spiritual heritage outranks biological lineage. After all, genetics last for eighty years; spiritual legacy lasts forever.

My great-grandfather James Cornish was a circuit-riding preacher in the Old West. I have his pulpit Bible from when he settled down to pastor a frontier church in Kansas. It includes family records going back to our roots in Cornwall. (My name reflects our heritage to this day.)

Cornwall is a windswept peninsula jutting into the Atlantic from southwest Britain, where my earliest ancestors were probably Celtic warriors and Druid priests. If some of them came to Christ, I hope they didn't become Pelagian on their spiritual journey through Celtic Christianity, and I hope their descendants became Puritans. If you don't know the differences among those groups, or if you can't rank them according to their scriptural faithfulness, this book should help.

While I've never been to Cornwall, I like to read the history of the Cornish people. But what lasting benefit do I or others gain from learning of human ancestry, other than a sense of pride mixed with occasional embarrassment? (In fairness to the dead, I wonder what embarrassment they would have on seeing us, their descendants!)

I can trace my spiritual ancestry through the family of a friend who brought me to Christ. I can even go back further to the family who evangelized *them.* But it ends there. I don't know who my spiritual great-grandparents are, and I'll probably never find out in this life. But I do know a little about the big picture of my spiritual family. All those in Christ from every nation and ethnic group over a period of two thousand years are part of that family—including you, I hope.

But why study church history? For starters, Christianity is life as well as truth. Those who came before us tried to live what we believe. If we learn their doctrine without its application, we miss half the picture. How did they approach life as the outgrowth of our shared truth? Also, even though dead, our spiritual ancestors help us interpret that truth. We don't blindly accept all their interpretations of Scripture, but we should pause if we find that our cherished opinions were barely known or even rejected by saints more godly than we. Church history also spotlights which doctrines and issues are central to the faith and which rightly belong to the fringes. Bowed before the steady gaze of history, we gain humility in how we hold our views.

We also draw a kind of reverse encouragement by hearing of the mistakes of those before us. By learning of their failures, we avoid their pitfalls. Or at least we should. Not everybody in the history of the church was saintly; some were scoundrels. How refreshing—you and I are not the only failures to follow Christ! Of course, marvelous examples of Christlike character and godly living abound in history as well. How motivating—we have models to aspire to! Millions of Christians have fallen in the middle, ordinary people who have tried by the grace of God to be faithful to Him but have never achieved enough to land in a book. That's most of us, at least most of the time, plodding along a well-worn path.

In heaven we'll be able to learn the history of each of Christ's followers firsthand. Because I love history, that alone will be heaven to me. In addition to listening to unrecorded details about Jesus' life from the Lord Himself, imagine doing the same with Moses and Daniel, Paul and Mark, Athanasius and Augustine, John Wycliffe and Jonathan Edwards, and many others. But we already know parts of their stories. It may be more fascinating to hear the accounts of unknown Christians from a fourth-century Egyptian desert or an eleventh-century European hut or a twentieth-century

Soviet labor camp. I look forward to hearing your story. You might be interested in mine.

But your story and mine don't end with us. Our part in church history continues in others who follow us. God will use you, and I hope me, to influence them for Him. You will meet people in heaven who lived on earth after you left it and who will trace their spiritual legacy to you. And they'll praise God for His grace to them through you. What will church history, when finished, record of our lives?

I wrote *5 Minute Church Historian* for the same reasons I wrote *5 Minute Theologian* and *5 Minute Apologist*. They originated as an idea for training my sons as thinking Christians and grew into three books at the urging of friends. I knew my boys wouldn't be taught church history in school or even in church or youth group, so I taught them myself. As with the previous two books in the 5 MINUTE series, the chapters here are intentionally short for busy people to read in five minutes. No fluff; just the facts.

The format should work for individuals, youth groups, and homeschoolers who want an introduction to church history. And, like the previous books, this one makes a quick, ready reference. But I believe it will help people of all ages, not just high school kids. After all, when most adult Christians think John Wycliffe started Wycliffe Bible Translators, we need a better grasp of church history.

This book is chronological. Part 1 (covering AD 30–313) records the first steps of the church, threatened by enemies on all sides, from shortly after Jesus' ascension until the early fourth century, when Emperor Constantine gave Christianity the official okay. In part 2 (313–590) we watch the way in which the church used its formal recognition to grow in power. We find a strong and united church in part 3 (590–1054) until tension over the growing power of the Bishop of Rome led the Eastern and Western Churches to split into what we now call Eastern Orthodoxy and Roman Catholicism. As a result, during the period covered in part 4 (1054–1517), two dominant branches— one Western, the other Eastern—developed in separate directions. Part 5 (1517–1563) covers the Reformation and its immediate aftermath in the West, while part 6 (1563–1648) portrays its lingering results. Human reason threatens divine revelation (in some circles) in part 7 (1648–1789), with an explosion of missionary activity following in part 8 (1789–1900). Parts 9 and 10 cover the twentieth century and the start of the twenty-first, divided by World War II.

Not all will agree with the hundred entries I chose as key people and events. My list records a small part of the stories of Christ's people who made a lasting difference: thinkers and theologians, missionaries and martyrs, and a few pastors and others. It also points to major events that shaped the church. More happened than New Testament goings-on, Luther stirring the pot, and Grandpa "getting religion." Some of the events included in this book are no longer well-known, but they all changed our world.

All Christians are molded by our shared heritage, and we, in turn, shape it. History teaches that one person can make a difference, and it points to the path where many before us have trod. I hope that *5 Minute Church Historian* motivates readers to dive into more substantial accounts of our spiritual legacy and find their own place on that path.

THE BEGINNING (AD 30–100)

Pentecost, Persecution, and Destruction

"I will build My church," said Jesus, "and the gates of hell shall not prevail against it" (Matthew 16:18, KJV). He was right. He started His church, and though it has endured hell on earth, it still exists today.

The first chapter of church history was written by the Holy Spirit through His servant Luke, a Gentile physician perhaps from Antioch in Syria. We call Luke's church history book, simply, Acts. How did the church start?

Seven weeks after Jesus' crucifixion and resurrection, Jews from across the Roman Empire gathered in Jerusalem for the festival of Pentecost. A group of 120 of Jesus' followers were meeting in a private home when the Holy Spirit came on them. They went to the streets, heading for the temple. A stunned crowd of foreign Jews collected to hear these Galileans speaking in many languages. (Galileans were not usually well educated.) Arriving at the temple, Peter preached a powerful message, and three thousand believed and were baptized. Thus the church began (Acts 1–2).

Over the next forty years the church spread at a furious pace, but success sparked persecution. The preaching of Stephen was too radical for the Jewish Sanhedrin, or high council, so the council members had him stoned (Acts 6:15–7:60). He thus became the first Christian martyr (at least that we know of). Widespread persecution followed, forcing the Christians to flee Jerusalem (8:1). But wherever they went, they spoke of the risen Christ and His saving work (verse 4).

A young Jewish scholar named Saul (later Paul) was largely responsible for this persecution (verses 1-3). But his efforts were interrupted when the risen Christ confronted him and he became a follower (9:1-22).

As the church spread from Judea across the empire, the potential for more persecution arose. Romans worshiped many gods, so they viewed Christians, who worshiped a single, invisible God, as atheists. Also, Christians, like Jews, refused to acknowledge the emperor's deity, further inviting the wrath of the state. The ingredients for widespread persecution were present. Meanwhile, trouble was brewing back home.

Jews and Romans barely tolerated each other, and in AD 66 the Jewish nation exploded in revolt. The Romans struck back by besieging Jerusalem. Finally, in the year 70, the siege of Jerusalem succeeded. The Roman army breached the walls of the Holy City and destroyed the temple. Nearly all the city's inhabitants were killed or scattered. Most Christians had already fled (an act of treason, according to Jews), and the divide between Christianity and Judaism was complete. The Christian headquarters moved north to Antioch in Syria, where God's Word was taught and missionary efforts aimed at Gentiles began (Acts 11:19-26; 13:1-4).

Most of the apostles had died by AD 70. Seasoned and scattered by persecution, the church entered the second century with new leadership but the same message and a bigger audience: the empire—and eventually, the world. The early church expected persecution, almost embraced it. They considered martyrdom the highest form of imitating Christ, who died for them. They "rejoic[ed] because they had been counted worthy of suffering disgrace for the Name" (Acts 5:41).

JUSTIN MARTYR (C. 100–165)

Nicknamed for Death

If you're killed for a cause, you're called a martyr. Most people wouldn't choose to die that way, but a second-century Christian named Justin is known for doing that. In fact, his name has come down to us as Justin Martyr.

Justin was born in Samaria to a non-Christian family and was raised as a pagan. As a young man, he pursued philosophy in his search for truth. He studied the Stoics, Aristotle, Plato, and others, but none satisfied his soul or answered his questions.

One day when he was about thirty, while walking by the sea, he met an old man who engaged him in conversation. After discussing God and other lofty issues, the man suggested a different path in the search for truth. He told Justin that some ancient prophets knew more about God than did the current-day philosophers, and he advised Justin to explore their writings. He did, and he found in these Old Testament prophets what he'd been searching for. They pointed to the true "philosophy" of Christ and Christianity.

He then started a school in Ephesus before moving to Rome. But God would use Justin's pen more than his classroom. His *1 Apology,* written about 155, was the first major scholarly defense of Christianity. About 160 he wrote two other works: *2 Apology,* addressed to the Roman Senate and people, and *Dialogue with Trypho the Jew.*

Justin addressed *1 Apology* to Emperor Antoninus Pius and his sons. His intent was to portray Christianity as reasonable and as no threat to the state, making the case that it should be treated as a legal religion. He argued that Christians shouldn't be condemned or punished for their convictions but only if they committed a crime. He also tried to disprove the charges of immorality leveled at Christians.

Justin wrote as a philosopher to philosophers, arguing from rational evidence that Christianity is true. He believed, however, that the mind alone cannot bring a person to God. According to Justin, revelation of the *Logos,* the living Christ, is the source of saving faith. Justin's style was gracious and respectful rather than harsh or argumentative.

But Emperor Marcus Aurelius (reigned 161–180) fiercely opposed Christianity. Blaming Christians for anything bad that happened in his empire, he ordered their persecution. About 165, Justin and some of his disciples were accused of being Christians, and Justin was charged with teaching an illegal religion. At their trial the Roman prefect asked if these things were true. They confessed and were scourged, then beheaded. Other believers called Justin "Martyr," and the name stuck.

He was not the first to argue that Christianity is true, but he was the first to engage other philosophies on their own terms. He communicated Christian truth in the language of his hearers. His influence is seen in later Christian thinkers, including Irenaeus, Tertullian, Origen, and Athanasius.

Justin Martyr set an example for us in how to communicate in the language of our listeners. When we share Christ with others, perhaps we should ask ourselves what Justin apparently did: *Are they hearing what I'm saying?*

Power in Dying

The apostle John spent his last years ministering in and around Ephesus. After his death, about the year 100, his disciples continued his work. One of them was Polycarp (c. 69–155), who pastored the church in nearby Smyrna (modern Izmir, Turkey).

We know little of Polycarp's birth, family, conversion, or life. We do know that early in the second century his ministry flourished among all classes of society. He also composed a letter (somewhat like Paul's) to the Philippian church, who previously had written questions to him. His fifty-year influence throughout Asia Minor was so powerful that he was known by his enemies as an atheist who destroyed their traditional gods.

His church recorded the story of his arrest, "trial," and martyrdom in a letter to other churches. Anti-Christian sentiment had spread across the province of Asia Minor, and riots erupted in Smyrna. When the authorities decided to kill some Christians, Polycarp's friends insisted that he hide on a farm outside town. He did, but soldiers tortured a servant into revealing his hiding place, and Polycarp was arrested. The authorities wanted a denial of the faith from this respected church leader more than they wanted his head.

His graciousness showed even while he was under arrest, as he served a meal to the officers who came to take him away. He also prayed for his friends, who would be crushed by his loss.

The dialogue between Polycarp and the governor is recorded in some detail. Standing in the crowded arena, the pastor was asked to swear allegiance to Caesar. He responded that he had served the Lord for eighty-six years and couldn't deny him now. The governor reminded him that wild animals waited nearby to tear him to pieces. Polycarp said to bring them on.

The governor replied that if he didn't want to be consumed by animals, a fire could be built to burn him alive. The soon-to-be martyr reminded the governor of God's eternal fire of judgment, which he would someday face. The fearless saint then prayed that God would accept his death as a sacrifice. The soldiers lit the fire, and he passed into the presence of his Lord.

God converted Polycarp's grace and strength in the face of death into a victory. The crowds were appalled at the execution of this honorable man. Apparently, enough was enough for even the most brutal among them, and the persecutions soon ended. His church annually celebrated his grace under fire, setting a precedent for some Christians to venerate the deaths of the saints.

Most Christians have wondered how they would respond if given the choice to deny Christ or die. For almost two thousand years, the church has held up Polycarp as the premier model of how to react in such circumstances. Because of Polycarp, as well as Christians who suffer and die for Christ today, we can draw courage to stand and speak more boldly for the Savior who bought us.

IRENAEUS (C. 130–200)

Refuting Heretics

Persecution from Rome was not the only challenge to the early church. Heresies from within soon tested the church's belief system. But God had people on hand to respond to the crisis. One was Irenaeus.

We know little of Irenaeus's life. He was born in Asia Minor, and when he was young he was exposed to Polycarp, possibly as his student. After visiting Rome, he settled at a government transportation center at Lyon, France. In 177 Emperor Marcus Aurelius targeted that region for persecution. When Pothinus, bishop of the Lyon church, was martyred, Irenaeus apparently assumed his post.

Irenaeus wrote several books, though only two of them survive. The first is a five-volume set known as *Against Heresies*. The other is *Proof of the Apostolic Preaching*, which ties the apostles' teaching and writings (the New Testament) to the Old Testament. *Against Heresies* was aimed primarily at a growing system called Gnosticism, which used Christian terms in unorthodox ways.

Gnostic beliefs varied, but their centerpiece was the idea that the material world, including our bodies, is evil and that only the spiritual, immaterial world is good. According to the Gnostics, a lower god, the god of the Old Testament, created the physical world as his domain. Our inner persons, or spirits, are good but are trapped within evil physical bodies. Christ came to free our spirits from these bodily prisons. Christ Himself didn't have a real physical body; He only looked as though He did. His plan was to teach us secret knowledge about our real spiritual Father, by which we escape our bodies and this world.

Irenaeus reminded his readers that anyone can use Scripture, as the Gnostics did, to defend their opinions. But teachings that deviate from the heritage passed down from the apostles need serious scrutiny. If the Gnostics's "truth" is from God, why did the apostles say nothing about it? Theologically, Irenaeus clarified central doctrines that refuted Gnostic beliefs. The Old and New Testaments reveal only one God, and Jesus is His unique Son, the eternal Word who became fully human. God created the physical world, including human bodies, and pronounced it good.

Gnosticism was not the only heresy Irenaeus tackled. A man named Marcion also thought the Bible revealed two Gods: a wrathful Old Testament God and a loving New Testament God. Driven by anti-Jewish bias, Marcion circulated his own canon of the New Testament, which included only Luke's Gospel and ten of Paul's letters. When Marcionite churches began to appear, Irenaeus wrote against that heresy too, again stressing the existence of one God and the unity between the testaments.

The impact of Irenaeus was not felt during his lifetime. Only with the insight of history did the church realize what he had achieved. His biblically based writings stabilized Christianity against the onslaught of heretical teachings, and his arguments set the direction for future theology. Tradition tells us that in about the year 200, many Christians were killed in Lyon, Irenaeus among them. We cannot be certain that this story is true, and in any case the details are unknown. Nevertheless, Irenaeus is considered a martyr.

We learn from Irenaeus that sound principles of interpretation should guide our study of the Bible. Wild-eyed speculation and picking and choosing what we want from Scripture are neither God's intent nor a part of the best heritage of the church.

A Sharp but Powerful Pen

In the second century, Rome increased its persecution of the church. But thinking Christians began to respond. They wrote brilliant works to counter the political powers and pagan philosophies of the day. One of the best of these apologists was Tertullian.

Tertullian was the son of a Roman centurion assigned to duty in Carthage, North Africa. His early life is a mystery to the pages of history, but we know that he was bright and well educated. He took his training in literature, law, and logic, resulting in knowledge of Greek and Latin expressed with a flair for airtight legal argument. Armed with this high-powered intellectual ammunition, he wrote in defense of the faith.

We don't know the details of Tertullian's conversion to Christianity. Some scholars speculate that he was so taken with the courage of Christian martyrs that he became a Christian as a result. Indeed his writings exalt martyrdom, perhaps supporting the conclusion that seeing their faith unto death led his faith unto spiritual life.

Tertullian began his literary defense of Christians in 197. He was a powerful and cutting writer, attacking almost everyone with whom he differed, both outside the church and within. His harsh, sarcastic style was the opposite of Justin Martyr's graciousness. His central point for those who opposed the church was that Christians were loyal to the state and should be left alone; Rome's persecutions were illegal.

He urged Christians to separate from pagan culture and philosophy. "What has Athens to do with Jerusalem?" he asked. In other words, what does worldly philosophy have to do with God's people? Interwoven within his apologetics we also find seminal ideas for the church's budding theology. Better than anyone before him, he explained the Trinity and the nature of Christ.

His unbending perfectionism eventually led to his own defection from the church. He joined the Montanists, an ascetic "Christian" offshoot that began in Asia Minor but wielded influence in Carthage. Montanists believed they received new revelation directly from the Spirit, thought the Lord was returning immediately to set up His kingdom, and required strict observance of dietary and other noncritical rules. (In 381 the Council of Constantinople condemned Montanism.)

Little is known of Tertullian's death. One tradition

says he lived to old age; another believes he received the prize of martyrdom. Either way, his mixed legacy lives on. His strength of conviction has been admired, but his heavy-handed style has met with condemnation. His thoughts on the Trinity and the nature of Christ formed the basis for the church's future understanding of those core doctrines. The great councils over the next two and a half centuries were guided by his insights.

May we strive to follow the strength, passion, and conviction of this great apologist. But, by God's grace, may we seek a gentle spirit, which Tertullian sometimes lacked. As Paul wrote in Ephesians 4:15, we ought to "[speak] the truth in love."

ORIGEN (C. 185–254)

The Iron Man

New York Yankee Lou Gehrig was known as the Iron Man for never missing a game in many years of playing baseball. Not until Cal Ripkin of the Baltimore Orioles came along did anyone play in more consecutive games. In a similar way, because of Origen's long and consistent writing career and his strength under torture, he was called the Iron Man.

Origen was educated in classics in his hometown of Alexandria, Egypt, the Roman Empire's center of learning and culture. He applied his brilliant mind to writing and produced eight hundred manuscripts, bringing Christianity to the forefront of intellectual respectability. At the same time, his allegorical interpretation of the Bible led to conclusions beyond the bounds of orthodoxy.

When the future scholar was seventeen, persecution broke out and his father, Leonidas, was arrested. Origen wrote him a letter in prison, urging him not to forsake the faith for the sake of his family. After his father's death, Origen sought martyrdom too, but his mother restrained his youthful vigor. The young genius became the family breadwinner, earning a meager living by teaching.

The same persecution drove the great teacher Clement from Alexandria and his school. So at the age of eighteen Origen was offered the post of principal, and he began his extraordinary career as a teacher, scholar, and writer. Still facing persecution, he simplified and disciplined his life to an extreme and threw himself into his work. He began writing about 215, producing more commentaries on the Bible than anyone else before the Reformation, thirteen centuries later. His amazing literary output was aided by a wealthy patron named Ambrose, who paid for a staff to write down, copy, and publish Origen's words.

Origen blended Christian theology with Greek philosophy. Influenced by Plato's ideas, he believed the Bible could be understood on three levels: (1) literally on the surface, (2) morally in the soul, and (3) allegorically to explore hidden mysteries. The final level was most important to him.

The ascetic life prepared Origen for his own earthly end. Emperor Decius targeted the great writer in the persecutions of 250. Decius wanted to force Christian leaders to recant their faith, so Origen was imprisoned and tortured. But he remained true to his Lord. Even though he was later released, he died three years afterward as a result of the brutal treatment.

Origen's legacy is mixed. His brilliance and productivity left an extraordinary influence on the church. He understood that Christianity must feed the mind as well as the heart. He wrote the first systematic theology *On First Principles*, some of which was later considered unorthodox. But the more offbeat ideas may have stemmed from disciples who took his thoughts beyond his intent.

Three centuries later, at the Second Council of Constantinople, Emperor Justinian led a movement to condemn and destroy some of Origen's books. By the standards of his own time, however, his views were not as unorthodox as they later appeared. The implications of his ideas didn't come to fruition until generations after him.

From Origen we learn caution about accommodating the Bible to the philosophy of the day. We also find an example for future scholars: the blend of a brilliant mind and a devoted heart. Intellect can be mixed with passion for the living God.

THE PERSECUTIONS OF DECIUS
AND DIOCLETIAN (250 AND 303)

Turning Up the Heat

Before the mid-third century, most of the persecution Christians endured resulted from random mob action, not government policy. That changed under the emperors Decius (reigned 249–251) and Diocletian (reigned 284–305). Rome took a more direct role, and persecution became government policy throughout the empire. For two and half centuries the church had been seen as a sect of Judaism, a legal religion. But no longer. Christians were clearly their own crowd and perhaps a threat to Rome, or so the government feared. The solution was simple: Get rid of them.

Decius ascended the throne when Rome was suffering social problems inside and attacks from the Goths outside. Christian worship of one God challenged the traditional Roman beliefs of polytheism as well as the veneration of emperors past and present. Because the Christian God was invisible, it was assumed that these social misfits had to be atheists. Decius concluded that an edict requiring everyone to sacrifice to the gods of Rome, combined with an order to seize those who refused, would raise moral standards.

Those who performed the sacrifice received a certificate proving their loyalty to the state. Those who did not could be imprisoned or killed. Many Christians gave in; others refused and were imprisoned, tortured, and executed. By God's grace, this persecution ended when Decius died in battle against the Goths one year later. The church would enjoy forty years of peace.

The disorder of the third century heightened the need for a strong leader, and Diocletian was the man for the job. He ascended from the military to inflict totalitarianism on the empire, trying to wipe out the church along the way. His motive is not clear, because for eighteen years he had seemed oblivious to Christians. Their numbers had grown to nearly 10 percent of the population, including his wife, his daughter, and many of his officials. But two years before the end of his reign, he ordered what came to be known as the Great Persecution. The effects were awful. As before, Christians had to sacrifice to the Roman gods. Furthermore, they were not allowed to meet, their buildings and Scriptures were destroyed, and their leaders were imprisoned.

The grandaddy of all persecutions began to subside soon after Diocletian retired in 305. His successor,

Galerius, one of the instigators of the nightmare, finally realized that the Christian faith could not be stamped out. The more Christians were tortured and killed, the more their faith spread. The public could stomach no more bloodshed. This last and worst of Roman persecutions officially ended in 311 when Galerius said, "No more."

Despite the worst that Rome could throw at the church, it survived and thrived as Jesus had promised. Even in tragedy God brings blessing. The unanticipated benefit in this horror was the church's realization of the need to identify the canon of Scripture—the list of writings the church would recognize as inspired by the Holy Spirit. If they were going to suffer and die for their books, Christians wanted to make sure they had the right ones.

We shouldn't be surprised that persecution persists today. Jesus said, "If they persecuted me, they will persecute you also" (John 15:20). He also promised, "Blessed are you when people insult you, persecute you and falsely say all kinds of evil against you because of me" (Matthew 5:11). May we remember Peter's words from 1 Peter 4:16: "If you suffer as a Christian, do not be ashamed, but praise God that you bear that name."

ST. ANTONY (C. 251–356)

The Father of Monasticism

Christian separation from the world — a principle taught in Scripture—has been understood and applied differently in various times and places. From the late third century, some believers separated by abandoning society. Either alone or in small communities, they gave up a normal life to more fully pursue such spiritual disciplines as solitude, prayer, and fasting, as well as reading and meditation on Scripture.

The early leader and premier example of the monastic life was Antony of Egypt. Almost everything we know about him comes from his biography, *The Life of St. Antony*, written by Athanasius in the 340s. Antony may not have been the first Christian hermit, but he was the first to be known for it, referred to by some as "the father of monasticism."

He was born into a well-heeled Christian family in the village of Koma, Egypt. But at about age eighteen, he lost his parents and assumed the care of his younger sister and the family estate. Soon thereafter, while on his way to church one Sunday, he was thinking of how the early Christians sold their possessions and gave the money to the poor (Acts 4:32-37). When the morning sermon was preached on the same topic, he was convinced that it was aimed at him, so he gave away the family estate and possessions, put his sister in a convent, and began the ascetic life of a hermit.

Antony launched his life of discipline not far from civilization so he could consult with other hermits. Above all, though, he desired the solitude to pray and pursue God, so when he gained a reputation among nearby villagers, who sought his wisdom, he moved further into the desert. After twenty years of isolation, fighting demons and temptation, he emerged from his solitude to find a crowd waiting for him. He graciously taught them what he had learned.

During his remaining years, he alternated between isolation and community involvement. (He once even traveled to Alexandria to aid Athanasius in his fight against the heresy of Arianism.) As a result of Athanasius's book, Antony's fame spread, and he established a monastery, which became the pattern for monasteries across Egypt.

A century later, his influence reached Augustine when the future giant of the faith recalled Antony's conversion experience during his own coming to Christ.

Antony's impact extended to untold ordinary Christians who never intended to pursue the monastic life. But they came to value solitude in the soul and discipline of the spirit. For a thousand years, he was idolized as the model monk and the inspiration for monasteries across the East and Europe.

Despite the rigors of his ascetic life, Antony lived 105 earthly years. He died with next to nothing, but as death drew near, he told friends to be sure to give his sheepskin cloak to Athanasius. No one knows where he's buried; his grave was unmarked.

Antony desired to know and serve Christ without distraction. And he found that the soul grows strong when physical pleasures are denied. Having less clutter of stuff and less chaos of time can unclog our spiritual plumbing, while having too many things and too much busyness hinders intimacy with God. More than likely we won't want to go to Antony's extremes, but we can learn from his life that simplicity has the power to liberate us and make us more receptive to God.

Freedom of Religion

Early persecution couldn't kill the Jesus movement. By the fourth century, the church permeated the Roman Empire; but it soon learned that if the state grants freedom to exist, it may intervene in church affairs. The hinge of history turned when Emperor Constantine was converted to faith in Jesus Christ and issued the Edict of Milan, granting freedom of religion to all, including Christians. The age of martyrs ended, more or less, and the first steps toward a "Christian empire" were taken.

Constantine was born in the Balkans in the 270s to a Roman military officer and his wife. His father would eventually rise to the rank of Caesar (vice emperor at the time) over Britain and Gaul. As the son of a Caesar, Constantine was on the shortlist to someday become emperor himself. So, for his own career development, he was sent to serve as an official in the East.

In 306 Constantine's father died, and his army declared Constantine his successor. Six years later Constantine marshaled his troops ten miles north of Rome to engage the forces of Maxentius. Constantine appealed to whichever god would help him win the war. The night before the battle, he saw a vision of the cross in the sky, and he took it as a sign that he should display the Christian symbol on his banners and enter the fight with trust in the Christian God. The next day, he routed his enemy and became ruler of the western half of the empire.

Was Constantine truly converted, or was he merely an opportunist? We can't be sure. We do know that he never learned much Christian doctrine, and he wasn't baptized until shortly before his death in 337, although that was common at the time. He did embrace monotheism and defended the church. In 313 he and Licinius, ruler in the East, met in Milan, Italy, and issued an edict that changed the world. It gave freedom of worship to all, authorized the existence of churches, and returned Christians' property taken under Diocletian a decade before.

But freedom proved a mixed blessing. Constantine called himself the bishop of bishops and the thirteenth apostle. He considered the church to be under his rule. Because official authority now blessed the church, the unconverted masses swarmed in. The church of true believers became mixed with almost anyone who showed up. The wheat and the weeds occupied the same field as never before. And the foundation was laid for the medieval church, which tied religion and politics, money and power, into a knot that no one could undo for twelve hundred years.

Questions about the preferred relationship between church and state have hounded Christians for centuries. If government grants freedom, what will it want in return? Which is better: the state's cursing or its blessing? In our world, the church dwelling in freedom (as in America) often fades in influence as it assimilates to the surrounding culture, while the church dwelling under persecution (as in China) frequently flourishes as it did in the ancient world. Christians and people of all faiths desire freedom of religion, but the question remains: At what cost?

The Father of Church History

Christianity is grounded in the history of real events and people, not in the imaginary stories of myths and legends. The first Christian historian by any modern definition was Luke. Even among non-Christians, he is known as a first-rate historian. In the prologue of his gospel (Luke 1:1-4), he says that he thoroughly researched the existing accounts as background for his Spirit-inspired record of Jesus and the early church (Luke and Acts).

The title "father of church history," however, goes to Eusebius, the first to write Christian history on a broad scale. His *Ecclesiastical History* is our only source for many Christian events from the end of the apostolic age to the early fourth century. He is also known for his flattering biography of Emperor Constantine, which raised the question among modern historians of whether what he wrote was history or journalism or political propaganda.

Eusebius was born about 263, probably in Caesarea, Palestine. He was trained by Pamphilius, a scholar from Alexandria who was later martyred for his faith.

Pamphilius had collected a sizable library, including many of Origen's works, which Eusebius devoured.

Eusebius lived during an era of profound changes. From surviving prison and exile during the persecution of Diocletian, to sitting next to the emperor at the Council of Nicaea, he saw it all. Soon after he returned from exile (c. 303), the bishop in Eusebius's hometown of Caesarea died. Eusebius assumed his office and began a writing career. At the Council of Nicaea (325), he was sympathetic to the Arian position, but he later wrote a creed of his own and cleared himself of the charge of heresy. Perhaps aided by his friendship with the emperor, Eusebius was later offered the powerful position of bishop of Antioch. He turned it down, however, to remain in his smaller, less demanding post in Caesarea and devote more time to writing.

Eusebius gave us an inside view of the church in the early fourth century, presenting secular events from a Christian viewpoint. To this day he remains our best source of church history during its first three centuries. He also quoted extensively from other writings, thus preserving for us what would otherwise have been lost.

Like many Christians in different times and places, including today, he was blinded by his own culture and erroneously thought that the church of his time was what the church had always been. Thus he wrote little about how and why the church had changed since the apostolic age.

As historian and apologist, theologian and exegete, orator and political insider, Eusebius was a precursor of the universal man of the Renaissance, a thousand years yet in the future. His comments on politics paved the way for the Byzantine Empire, the medieval Christian world that survived the fall of Rome by a millennium. By modern standards of historical research and writing, his work lacked objectivity and analysis. But its positive traits made it the model for other church historians for centuries to come. Without him, we would be in the dark about early church history as it moved toward what is now called the Dark Ages.

One Word Makes All the Difference

Mark Twain believed that attention to details in writing is essential. He said, "The difference between the almost right word and the right word is really a large matter—it's the difference between the lightning bug and the lightning." The same holds true in theology.

Emperor Constantine wanted the Edict of Milan to unify Roman society. But the church itself was not as united as he had hoped. After the persecutions of Diocletian ended, and after Constantine's Milan-born freedom arrived, Christians' energy turned to theological dispute. At times the in-house quarreling grew so bitter that Christians themselves disturbed the newfound social peace. As some have said in our own day, "There's no war like a church war." What sparked this brawl among the followers of Christ?

For several years before Milan, Pastor Arius of Alexandria was teaching that Christ was not fully God. He said that Jesus was neither eternal nor omnipotent, and thus He did not possess the same nature as the Father. Christ was, in fact, a created being, a sort of super-angel, more than mere humanity but less than deity. After being created by the Father, Christ then created everything else. (This view is similar to that held by Jehovah's Witnesses today.) Alexander, the local bishop, and his friend Athanasius would have none if it, and the fight was on.

Emperor Constantine was no theologian, but news of turmoil in Alexandria caught his ear. He summoned church bishops to the little town of Nicaea, not far from Constantinople, to settle the issue and restore the peace of the church. In 325 about three hundred bishops, some of them bearing scars from the Great Persecution, arrived in Nicaea, and the proceedings began under the emperor's watchful eye.

Constantine began by reading letters from bishops about the Arian issue and urging them to find a path toward unity. Many were willing to compromise on the nature of Christ, but Athanasius refused, demanding a statement supporting Christ's complete deity. At one point the Arians blew their case by reading a statement directly denying the deity of Christ. The majority of the bishops were aghast. Any confusion there may have been about the Arian view disappeared.

The debate raged on and eventually swung on one statement: Christ is true God of true God, begotten of the Father, not made by the Father, and He is of "one substance" with the Father. All but two bishops signed on, and the issue was settled, at least for the time being. Orthodoxy carried the day by one word.

Indeed, one letter in the Greek language is the difference between "one substance" and "similar substance," the difference between full deity and something like (but less than) full deity. Details do make a difference. Even though the debate continued for a century, the Nicene Creed laid the foundation for the orthodox view on the nature of Christ in almost every variety of the church worldwide. When Christians today grow frustrated with theological thought and doctrinal precision, we might remember the difference that can be made by one word, even one letter. We can thank God for those who give their lives to getting the details of God's truth right.

One Against the World

Most of us have answered a knock on the door to find a pair of Jehovah's Witnesses ready to engage us in battle over the deity of Christ. They are well versed on the issue and may sound convincing if we allow them to twist the Scriptures to their liking. Non-Christians and untrained Christians can be subverted by their clever tactics, concluding that their newfound friends have discovered truth that the rest of the church missed.

But this battle was already fought in the fourth century. The champion of orthodoxy was a young scholar from Alexandria, a short black man named Athanasius. We know little of his background except that he was born in Alexandria about 296 and educated at the Christian school there. At twenty-three he was ordained a deacon by Bishop Alexander, whom he assisted at the Council of Nicaea, called to decide the Arian issue.

When Alexander died in 328, Athanasius succeeded him. For forty-six hard years he served as bishop of Alexandria. He endured false charges that ranged from witchcraft to murder. Seventeen years of his ecclesiastical rule were spent away from his home and church as a result of five different exiles, mostly stemming from imperial politics. But his character was resolute: If need be, he would stand against the empire and the whole world in defense of truth.

Three of his books stand out. *The Life of St. Antony* altered Western Christianity for centuries by spreading monasticism across Europe. As a result of this wildly popular book, people believed that the virtuous Christian life was found among the hermits in the desert. *On the Incarnation* explains the early church's understanding of redemption and the need for the incarnation of Jesus to attain it. By it we are re-created as God intended us to be. *Against the Arians* argues for the full deity of Jesus Christ. He was not, as the Arians contended, created by the Father but rather was co-equal and co-eternal with the Father. Athanasius had persuasively debated this position at Nicaea, championing the view destined to become orthodoxy.

Another notable entry on his résumé is his recognition of the twenty-seven New Testament books that eventually won the church's acceptance as divinely inspired. As far as we know, his Easter letter of 367 was the first record of the exact list of New Testament books we use today, and they appear in the same order.

Athanasius died in office at the age of seventy-five. But his views of the Trinity were still not fully developed or accepted by all Christians. That work was left for those yet to come, the Cappadocian Fathers. He had, however, laid the foundation on which they would build the doctrine that orthodox Christians still hold today.

Even Augustine viewed Athanasius as a hero of the faith. The controversial theologian of Africa suffered greatly for truth, remaining unbending in the face of criticism, rejection, and imperial opposition. One-third of his career as bishop was served in exile or on the run.

Christians today need courage to stand for truth despite the cost. What the crowd says and how it acts should not determine our path. Few modern Christians have heard of Athanasius, but he is one of the first they should find in heaven and give their thanks to.

The Big Three

Despite the conclusion of Nicaea, Arianism persisted. After Athanasius died in 373, God used a threesome from Cappadocia in central Turkey to fight for orthodoxy. Basil of Caesarea, his best friend, Gregory of Nazianzus, and his younger brother, Gregory of Nyssa, are known as the Cappadocian Fathers because of their homeland. Their lasting impact made its big splash in 381 at the Council of Constantinople, which confirmed the Son's deity and stated the Spirit's deity. Thus neither the Son nor the Spirit is subordinate to the Father; all three equally and eternally share the same essence.

Basil the Great (c. 330–379) was born into a wealthy Christian family. While attending school in Athens, he met Gregory, soon to be his lifelong friend. In 356 he completed his studies and returned to his home city of Caesarea. But rather than pursue a secular career as did his lawyer father, he took his older sister's advice and chose the ascetic life, eventually becoming Caesarea's archbishop in 370.

Basil penned the first book ever written solely about the Holy Spirit, arguing for the Spirit's full deity. He was thus known as "the theologian of the Holy Spirit." He founded his own monastery, and his rules for monastic discipline still guide Greek Orthodox monks. On New Year's Day 377 or 379 he died, too soon to see his work fully accepted at the great council of 381. But his ideas prevailed, and he is known as Basil the Great.

Gregory of Nazianzus (c. 330–389) was also born into wealth, near the Cappadocian city of Nazianzus (thus the name). Basil urged him to accept the position of bishop, which he did, but this shy, scholarly man yearned for a secluded life of study and writing. The books he wrote argued persuasively for the Trinity, preparing the church for the coming council. By then the great Basil was dead. So, at the behest of Emperor Theodosius, Gregory led the council for a short time. But criticism and possibly Arian threats led to his resignation.

Nevertheless, his legacy lives on. The wording of the Nicene Creed, used from the fifth century on, probably came from this council and is thought by some to be the baptismal confession Gregory used in his church. He retired and died on the family estate about 390.

His profound thinking earned him the simple title "the theologian."

Gregory of Nyssa (c. 340–395) was trained by his brother, Basil, rather than in an official school, but his remarkable mind overcame his relative lack of education. For a few years he served as the bishop of Nyssa in western Cappadocia. After Basil's death, he bore the intellectual mantle of orthodox trinitarianism. Some scholars say he was one of the most brilliant thinkers in the early church. A mystic as well as a scholar, he helped form the mystical tradition that permeates the Eastern church even today.

Gregory wrote many works, using Greek philosophy to reveal the mystery of God. He contributed much to the Council of Constantinople, delivering the inaugural address, guiding it toward its pro-Nicene stance, and perhaps recording some of its conclusions. He died about 395.

The Cappadocian Fathers played a crucial role in the church's doctrinal development away from Arianism, affirming and clarifying the deity of the Spirit as well as the Son. These three men of vastly different temperaments were each used by God in unique ways. They show that God doesn't search for people with a certain personality before enrolling them in His service.

He desires a willing heart, surrendered to Him and His glory, His Word, and His work.

AMBROSE (C. 340–397)

Mentor of a Giant

Church history portrays Augustine as the giant of the fourth century, even the first millennium. Among the factors God wove together to draw him to Christ, Ambrose was most significant.

Ambrose was born into a prestigious Christian family, the son of Aurelius Ambrosius, governor of Britain, Spain, and Gaul. As a governor's son, he was educated in Rome, anticipating a career in government or some other public service.

He became a lawyer in 365, then governor of the area around Milan in northern Italy. When the local bishop died in 374, the people demanded that Ambrose fill his slot. Interpreting this public call as God's will, he gave away his wealth and immersed himself in study to prepare for his new vocation. He became the leading preacher of the Western church, a contemporary of the greatest of all: John Chrysostom in the East. Theologically, he paved the way for Augustine's development of the idea that original sin is the main source of transgression even among Christians. In addition to pastoring an influential church, Ambrose became confidant and adviser to the emperor's family, who lived in Milan.

At that time in history, Christianity was the official religion of the Roman Empire. If you were Roman, you were Christian—or you better be. "Believers" received rewards; unbelievers were penalized. Emperors began to see their will and God's as one. But Ambrose opposed such a notion. When Emperor Theodosius ordered the slaughter of seven thousand people in Thessalonica over a minor political matter, Ambrose responded by excommunicating him. After some delay, the emperor repented and publicly apologized. The bishop had struck a courageous blow against the power of government to rule the church. That would not happen, at least not fully, on his watch.

The biggest feather in Ambrose's cap was not his restraint of the emperor's power but his influence on Augustine. As professor of rhetoric at the University of Milan, Augustine went to hear the great preacher Ambrose. Perhaps, Augustine thought, he could pick up some pointers from Ambrose's style. But the sermons' substance as well as their eloquence seized Augustine's heart. The Spirit wielded His truth on the future giant of the church. Augustine discovered that Christianity mixed brains with literary beauty, and he was hooked.

The studious Ambrose, a man of the Spirit and politics, multicultural and bilingual in Greek and Latin, also initiated hymn singing in the Western church, even writing some hymns of his own. His books *On the Faith* and *On the Holy Spirit* set the direction for Catholic theology. His impact was so substantial, in fact, that he's still known as one of the four doctors of the Western church—a title of scholarly distinction he shared with Jerome, Augustine, and Gregory the Great.

Ambrose's example should make us contemplate our influence on others. Our lasting legacy may not come through our own efforts as much as through our effect on someone who follows in our footsteps, someone we impact for Christ. We never know who we might shape for a future generation and for eternity.

The Greatest Preacher

In an age of great preachers, the greatest was John Chrysostom (Greek for "golden mouth"). He was born into a socially connected Christian family, the son of a government official in Antioch. As a leading intellectual center, Antioch offered the best education. John studied classics, law, and rhetoric under Libanius, a famous pagan orator, and theology under Diodorus of Tarsus.

The ascetic life appealed to John, and after his widowed mother died, he lived for two years in a cave, memorizing the New Testament. The rigors of the solitary life damaged his body but grew his soul. In time he turned from seclusion to serve in the church and was eventually appointed bishop of Antioch.

The common people loved his preaching, which condemned the excesses of the wealthy and the power of the elite. The rich and famous were predictably offended and therefore opposed John—a pattern that plagued him for life. But despite his refusal to play politics, his pulpit excellence could not be ignored. In 397 the emperor forced John to become bishop of Constantinople, the seat of imperial government, known as the New Rome.

But even in the shadow of the emperor, John would kowtow to no one. He preached against abuse of power in government and wealth in the church. He even took on the ruling family, comparing Empress Eudoxia to Jezebel. His verbal condemnations, simple lifestyle, and use of church money to build a hospital for the poor led to his demise. In 403 he was condemned, deposed as bishop, and forced into exile, leading to riots in the streets—a testimony to his popularity among the masses. While exiled to a remote part of the empire, he died from malnutrition and exposure.

John's handling of Scripture was driven by his belief in the divine inspiration of the Bible. God intended every word; thus each word carries His meaning. And so John sought to convey to his hearers the author's meaning in each text, and especially, to show how each text applied to everyday Christian life.

Eight hundred of John's sermons survive, more than those of any other church father. He usually taught verse by verse through entire books, introducing each with a message on the author and audience, setting and purpose, outline and theme. He aimed at two goals: understanding the literal meaning of the text and applying it to motivate his hearers toward change in their behavior. Learning and living God's Word formed the bedrock of John's ministry. The common folk so loved his preaching that he occasionally had to ask them to stop applauding. They wanted him to preach more and longer, even though his messages often lasted two hours.

John Chrysostom's legacy covers the theological spectrum. Many Eastern Orthodox churches are named after him, and his sermons, especially those on Paul's letters, affected the Reformation by influencing Luther and Calvin. The earthly reward for this prophetic preacher was exile and death. But he left an example of studying and teaching Scripture without twisting its meaning into something it's not. He satisfied the souls of his people without tickling their ears—a model for all who teach God's Word today.

JEROME (C. 345–420)

A Scholar's Scholar

Few people today value the writings of antiquity, known as the classics. But there was a time not long ago when knowing Greek or Latin was the sign of being an educated person. And many thinkers of the early church were trained in classical languages as tools for understanding the Bible, which was written in Hebrew and Greek.

One of the best of these thinkers was Jerome, the consummate scholar-monk who consumed ancient writings as easily as we read the newspaper. Some have called him the finest Latin writer of his day. In the late fourth century, Christianity was legal, almost mandatory, and the masses flooded the church, seeking to learn what it taught. So Bible scholars were in high demand, and men like Jerome filled the bill.

After completing his formal training in Rome, he moved to Syria in 372 to learn the monastic disciplines and study Hebrew from the desert monks. He later served for two years as secretary to Damasus, bishop of Rome. During that time, Jerome also acted as spiritual adviser to several prominent Roman families. By 386 he was back in the East, leading a monastery near Bethlehem, where he stayed for the rest of his life. September 30, the day he died in 420, is still known as St. Jerome's Day.

The Greek of the East was no longer known by many in the West. Because Latin was the common language, several attempts to translate the Bible from Greek into Latin had been undertaken. But none of the products was very good, so Bishop Damasus asked Jerome to produce an accurate Latin translation. He agreed and labored for twenty-three years to complete the massive task. The resulting masterpiece, called the Vulgate, became the authorized version of the Bible for Roman Catholicism until recent times. The quality was so high that Martin Luther, a thousand years later, quoted the Vulgate even though he knew the original languages.

As if that were not enough, Jerome also wrote commentaries on the biblical text, immersed himself in the theological struggles of the day, and corresponded with numerous people, including Augustine.

Jerome's legacy as a scholar is unsurpassed. Even Augustine believed that Jerome was one of the great scholars of the time. Centuries would pass before anyone's knowledge of the Bible equaled his. The growth of monasticism in the West during the Middle Ages was largely due to his writings about it. His model of using the original languages remains the standard for all translation work.

Jerome earned an international reputation as a scholar. He possessed the knack for researching and using the best insights from other scholars and schools of thought while avoiding their errors. He devoted himself to the Bible because he knew that only in its pages do we find the living Word, the source of life. Modern Christians seeking to restore their passion for Scripture would do well to look to Jerome as a model.

A Bad Boy, a Great Man

A scholarly mind and a pastoral heart are not always wed in a single person. But they were in Augustine, regarded as the greatest theologian of the first millennium and loved as a devoted pastor. He was born in 354 in Thagaste in northern Africa. He was, however, neither African nor European but Numidian, a descendant of an earlier, largely unknown race.

Augustine was raised by a Christian mother, Monica, but as a boy, he was a thief and a liar, hating school and often being punished for misbehavior. At age twelve he was sent to school in nearby Madaura and developed two interests that revealed his passionate soul. One was a love of learning; the other was lust. When he was sixteen, a wealthy friend paid for his further education at Carthage. The city's pagan attractions overcame his mother's warnings, and Augustine's lust found full expression. So did his passion for learning. He poured himself into such diverse fields as Latin, rhetoric, mathematics, music, and philosophy.

Augustine's quest for knowledge developed into a

search for wisdom in ancient religions. After converting to the Persian Manichean cult, he traveled to Rome and became famous as a lawyer but was soon hired by the University of Milan as professor of rhetoric. The pastor of Milan was Ambrose, a man of saintly character who possessed a preaching ability that even Augustine envied. Ambrose demonstrated that one could be an articulate intellectual and a Christian. Augustine admired being articulate and an intellectual, and he began to rethink the Christian position.

He became convinced that Christianity was true, but he was not ready to commit until a summer day in 386. While sitting and thinking under the shade of a fig tree, he heard a child singing the phrase "Take up and read." He knew neither the song nor its meaning, but he opened a Bible and read from Romans: "Let us behave decently, as in the daytime, not in orgies and drunkenness, not in sexual immorality and debauchery, not in dissension and jealousy. Rather, clothe yourselves with the Lord Jesus Christ, and do not think about how to gratify the desires of the sinful nature" (13:13-14). Convicted of sin, he came to Christ for forgiveness.

Augustine returned to North Africa and pursued a monastic life of prayer, study, and reflection. But in 391 the Christians in the town of Hippo virtually forced him to be their pastor. Reluctantly, he agreed and served them with such loving care that four years later he was elevated to the status of bishop. Even then, he continued his frugal lifestyle and objected to receiving special gifts or treatment. His most demanding pastoral challenge was to comfort his distressed flock when the capitol of their empire, Rome, was overrun and pillaged by barbarians. He urged his people to help the fleeing refugees rather than worry about their own fate.

In the midst of pastoral duties, Augustine never stopped applying his remarkable mind to God's Word. As he maintained a vigorous debate with the British heretic Pelagius over the doctrine of salvation, he also taught the Scriptures to his own people. Until his death in 430, he was a master of seeing the events of life in the light of God's Word.

Augustine modeled the thinking shepherd and was the bridge between ancient and medieval theology. He greatly influenced the Reformation of the sixteenth century and still guides theologians today. He remains a wonderful example of how truth and love can be mixed in a single soul.

PATRICK (C. 389–461)

Neither Catholic nor Irish

People wear green and march in parades to honor St. Patrick, the patron saint of Ireland. But he was neither Irish nor Roman Catholic. What we know of Patrick is a mix of fact and legend, but the truth reveals a genuine man of God.

Patrick was born to a Christian family about 389, the son of a civil servant in the Roman province of Britain. By the late fourth century, the Roman legions had abandoned Britain, leaving it vulnerable to Celtic invaders from Ireland. At the age of sixteen he was captured by slave traders plundering Britain's west coast. He was sold to an Irish farmer, for whom he tended pigs. During his six-year captivity, he reflected on his life and the Christianity he had been taught as a boy. His faith grew, and he yearned to be free.

Patrick was told in a dream that his ship was waiting. He escaped to the coast, where he boarded a vessel carrying a cargo of hounds to France. His pig-herding résumé became his ticket as he was given free passage for tending the dogs. Disembarking in France, he found his way to an island off the French Riviera where he joined a monastery.

Eventually, Patrick returned to Britain and his family. But his life was changed when he received another dream, similar to Paul's vision of the Macedonian man (Acts 16:9-10). In Patrick's dream, the Irish begged him to bring the gospel to the land of his former captivity. He was willing to obey but needed to prepare, so he studied at a monastery in Gaul.

In time he returned to Ireland and worked among the Celts despite opposition from their Druid priests. Only by faith in God's superior power did he prevail against their death threats. Their magical powers were real and the spiritual battle was intense. Meanwhile, Patrick's progress was slow, and many of his converts reverted to paganism. He focused on winning tribal kings to Christ, believing he would gain the people too. As he did, he spread the love of learning and the monastic way of life. The sons of converted kings became monks in the monasteries and priests of the churches he planted. After thirty years of ministry, he died in Ireland.

Before Patrick, a smattering of Christianity existed in the British Isles, probably left by Christians in the old Roman legions before they withdrew. But after Patrick, Christianity was firmly entrenched. Historians estimate that he planted two hundred churches and baptized one hundred thousand converts. He started Irish monasticism—the light that preserved civilization and the ancient texts through the Dark Ages. Reflecting a sense of divine justice, Patrick also ended the Irish slave trade. Following in his footsteps, hundreds of Celtic monks left their homeland over the next two centuries to take the gospel to Western Europe.

This humble man loved God deeply and devoted himself to prayer, Scripture, and service. Despite his "success," he viewed himself as a simple sinner. He showed remarkable courage in serving God and the people who had enslaved him as a youth. Patrick's example of faith, forgiveness, and sacrifice can guide us all as we strive to walk in the Master's steps.

Who Was Christ?

The councils of Nicaea (325) and Constantinople (381) affirmed the deity of Christ, but questions remained. If Christ is God, then how is He also a man? How do deity and humanity exist in one person? Is His deity complete or partial? Is His humanity like ours or something more, somehow mixed with deity? How do these two natures relate: is He one person or two, or a hybrid of both? When John wrote, "The Word became flesh" (1:14), what exactly did he mean?

Many opinions bounced about the church, but three got the most press. First, Apollinarius said the divine Word replaced and controlled Jesus' human mind and spirit. Only His body was human—a physical shell guided by the inner, divine Word. So Apollinarius gave up Jesus' humanity to keep His unity. Second, Nestorius maintained Christ's full deity and full humanity. But he went overboard, almost finding two separate persons in Jesus: one human, one divine. So Nestorius surrendered Christ's unity. Third, Eutyches tried to solve the problem by merging Christ's humanity into His deity. Thus he retained Christ's deity and unity but lost His humanity.

In May of 451, Emperor Marcian invited church bishops to Chalcedon, near his capital in Constantinople. He hoped they would settle the issue of who Christ is, but they wisely avoided trying to fully explain the mystery. In a series of fifteen meetings, the five hundred bishops affirmed the previous councils, then added something new: Christ is one person with two natures, truly God and truly man without mixture or loss of the traits of either nature.

This conclusion represented the high point of the church's expression of who Jesus Christ is, and it laid the cornerstone for the way we talk about Christ up to the present day. Against the Apollinarians, the bishops defended Christ's full humanity. Against the Nestorians, they protected His unity. Against the Eutychians, they rejected the merger of Christ's two natures into one.

From then on, Roman Catholics, Protestants, and most Eastern Orthodox accepted the results of Chalcedon. But some in the East did not. In Syria, the Nestorian Church rejected it, as their name implies. The Coptic Church of Egypt and Ethiopia also broke from the Eastern Orthodox Church over this issue. This formation of the Monophysite ("one nature") branch of the church reflects the first major split in church history, six centuries before the great division between Roman Catholic and Orthodox churches.

The great councils of Nicaea, Constantinople, and Chalcedon don't answer all our questions on the Trinity and Christ. But they set ground rules that separate orthodoxy from heresy. Chalcedon was the last council accepted by all major branches of Christendom, and it marks the end of the patristic age—the time of the church fathers. From this time forward, the church increasingly showed signs of becoming what we now call "medieval."

Chalcedon illustrates pastors at their best—thinking and learning what Scripture says about the doctrines that affect our lives and determine our destinies.

Writer of the Rule

During the Dark Ages, government and church conspired to hinder the exchange of ideas. As a result, the intellectual life of Europe almost died. But the love of learning was kept alive in the monasteries as monks preserved and copied the Scriptures, the works of the church fathers, and other writings of antiquity. While barbarians overran the empire, civilization crossed the bridge of monasticism connecting the ancient masters to the Renaissance and the Reformation.

For a thousand years, monasteries, more than churches, nurtured spiritual life. Monastic spirituality was rigorous. It required training; training meant discipline; and discipline needed rules. None wrote those rules better than Benedict.

Benedict was born in Nursia, eighty-five miles northeast of Rome, and was sent to the capitol to receive his training. But when he arrived, he was shocked by what he found: a degraded society far from the ideals of Christ. So the future "patriarch of Western monks" ran for the hills to pursue the ascetic life.

For three years he lived in a cave, studying Scripture, praying, and living a life of self-denial. The monks of a nearby monastery were so impressed by his devotion that they urged him to become their abbot. He did, but they found his discipline too austere and tried to poison him. Benedict got the hint and returned to the solitary life.

Benedict's ascetic life attracted more disciples, so in 529 he founded the now-famous monastery at Monte Cassino. He researched the spiritual wisdom of previous centuries, including that of St. Antony, the father of monasticism, and Augustine, the great African thinker and theologian. He learned much from a document known as the *Rule of the Master* and then wrote his own Rule, a manual for monasteries, destined to become the standard for centuries to come. The genius of his Rule was balance. He knew human nature, so he tempered monastic zeal with moderation.

Benedict's Rule appealed to ordinary men and women as well as super-saints and ascetic heroes. He believed that leadership of a monastery should be vested in a single abbot elected by the monks. The world beyond the cloistered walls posed spiritual danger, so monastic life would be withdrawn inside. Safely within the monastery, finding freedom from distraction, monks traveled the spiritual journey through Scripture, prayer, and service. They gathered to pray seven times a day, read and copied the Latin classics, and worked at manual labor, thus providing for the needs of the monastery.

Over the years, as Western monasticism changed, Benedict's Rule remained the standard instruction. His monastery at Monte Cassino survived until it was bombed during World War II. Monasteries preserved the best of the ancient world during the sometimes-brutal medieval era and affected Western religious life and society forever.

Modern people often point out monastic excesses, and they did exist. But most of these imbalances were no worse than ours today in the opposite direction. Who are we to condemn extreme self-denial in the pursuit of God if we exercise extreme self-indulgence in the pursuit of pleasure? Despite the monks' errors, perhaps we can look at their discipline and learn to live a more orderly and holy life.

CELTIC CHRISTIANITY
(SIXTH AND SEVENTH CENTURIES)

The Light of Ireland

In the fifth and sixth centuries, barbarians overran Europe, but Ireland was spared. As the continent fell into the abyss, Celtic Christians preserved the life of the mind and the spirit. Along with the monasteries of Europe, the Celtic church would shine as a bright light during the Dark Ages. Civilization survived— barely—because of it.

The dominance of the Roman Church was spreading, but Celtic Christianity flourished on its own. Geographically isolated from the rest of the world, these Christians followed a different path from that of believers in the church that was becoming the mother church of the West. The gospel didn't come to Ireland from Rome, and the Celts weren't about to submit to her. The independent spirit of Celtic Christians was a constant irritant to Rome, since the Roman bishop was accepted by many other people as the pope.

Celtic distinctives included bishops without established jurisdictions, a different date for Easter, and their monks' peculiar habit of shaving the front half of the head. But Celtic beliefs were orthodox. Their theology reflected the thinking of Basil, John Cassian, Jerome, Augustine, and Athanasius, whose writings were found in the libraries of Irish monasteries.

As barbarians burned and looted Europe, the Irish were becoming literate. They loved learning and books, which they beautifully illustrated. They copied and protected all the classics they could find, preserving the history and great ideas of the past. The world of books that Europe would someday become was largely due to Irish monks. Their scholarly passion was so intense that some of them even became advisers to royalty.

The Irish church loved missions as much as books, and Irish Christians took the gospel everywhere. They believed that voluntary exile for the gospel was a sign of spirituality, and they became the dominant missionary force in Western Europe for two centuries. They began in the far north of Scotland and moved south as far as Cornwall, eventually crossing the Channel to France, Germany, Austria, Switzerland, and northern Italy. Even Iceland wasn't immune from their missionary fervor.

Their two most celebrated missionaries were Columba (c. 521–597) and Columbanus (c. 550–615). Columba established monasteries in Scotland and

England, including the celebrated monastic community of Iona, a tiny island off Scotland's western coast. By the time he died, Columba was recognized as a poet and scholar as well as an innovative leader. Columbanus was a traveler who left Ireland to set up monasteries in France and Italy. As many as sixty grew from his initial work. He was known as a hothead who had run-ins with kings and popes, but he was one of the most effective evangelists Western Europe ever saw.

God greatly used the Irish church, but only for a while. The Vikings recorded their first raid of an Irish monastery in 793. They returned again and again and began to settle in the northern British Isles for easier access to larger and richer monasteries farther inland. By the late ninth century, Viking settlements were permanent, but as they merged with Irish society, they were in turn conquered by Christianity. By the next century, the Irish church had ceased as a separate entity from Rome, but we can still see its footprints on our world.

GREGORY THE GREAT (C. 540–604)

The Power of the Pope

In the late sixth century, Europe staggered beneath the weight of invasion, famine, and plague. It seemed that hell had erupted, and the crumbling government was helpless to fix the mess. The power vacuum was filled by the church, led by its pope. No one suddenly became pope (the position had been evolving for centuries), but many consider Gregory the first pope in the modern sense of the term.

Like so many other early church leaders, Gregory was born into a prominent family and trained for government service. He received the best available education, at a monastery in Rome, the city of his birth. Gregory's father hoped his son would follow him into civic duty, but when his father died Gregory gave his inheritance to the poor and converted his estate into a monastery.

Gregory wanted to live a simple life of scholarship and asceticism, but when he was only thirty-three Emperor Justin made him the mayor of Rome. In 579 the Roman bishop Pelagius II sent him as ambassador to Constantinople, seat of the Eastern empire. By the time he returned six years later, the people knew his abilities and wanted him as their bishop. He fled to escape their plans, but they found him and forced him into office in 590.

Gregory's achievements were extraordinary. In his younger years he had tried but failed to go to England as a missionary. But as pope, perhaps to compete with the Celtic church, he sent forty missionary monks to England under the leadership of Augustine (not to be confused with the great Augustine of North Africa). When the Lombards invaded, he raised troops, directed generals, and negotiated peace—all without government authorization. Assuming oversight of the Western church, he wrote *The Book of Pastoral Rule* and hundreds of personal letters to guide other bishops. He also made Benedict's Rule official policy for Western monasteries.

Gregory is regarded as one of the four doctors of the church, but not because he gave birth to new theological ideas. Rather, he made official the doctrines that grew into medieval Roman Catholicism. He also indirectly sparked the Reformation nine hundred years in the future because the beliefs he sanctioned inflamed Martin Luther, himself an Augustinian monk.

Some of those doctrines included the following:

humankind can cooperate with God to merit grace because we're not fully fallen; penance is an aid to forgiveness; we can pray to saints in heaven to help us on earth; holy relics hold divine power; we pass through purgatory before entering heaven; the Communion elements contain the literal body and blood of Christ; and church tradition is equal in authority to the Bible.

Gregory preferred the title "servant of the servants of God," but he was one of the most influential popes before the Reformation. By the time he died in 604, he was known as "God's consul," and the church would soon call him Gregory the Great. In the wake of his influence, government and society were soon dominated by the church in Rome, and that church was run by its bishop. The Western church was becoming the Roman Catholic Church, and Europe followed its lead. Gregory was the most significant person in that evolution. He exercised spiritual jurisdiction over churches in Italy, Gaul, Spain, Africa, and Britain, and he wielded powers previously held by the government. He was the pivot point of history between early and medieval Christianity.

Celts and Romans Collide

By the early fourth century, the Celtic church was so well established that it sent bishops to the Council of Arles in southern France in 314. Indeed, Celtic Christianity had prospered for centuries before the Roman Catholic Church began its mission to Britain. But Angles, Saxons, and Jutes invaded Britain in the early fifth century, driving the Celtic church westward into Wales, Cornwall, and Ireland and severing its contact with the outside world. How, then, did the Roman Catholic Church become involved in England?

In the late sixth century, when Gregory was still a monk, he saw a group of blond children being sold in a slave market in Rome. When he was told they were *Angli* (pagans from England), he said they looked like angels. He never forgot that scene, and in 596, as pope, he commissioned Augustine (head of St. Andrew's monastery in Rome, not Augustine the African bishop) to lead forty monks to the wild lands of England and convert Anglo-Saxon pagans to the Roman faith. Soon after they landed in 597, Augustine and his men won some converts, including Ethelbert, king of Kent, whose capitol was Canterbury. A year later Pope Gregory appointed Augustine to be the first bishop of Canterbury.

To his surprise, Augustine discovered Christians as well as pagans in Britain. As was the Roman custom, when he learned that some of their practices differed from those of Rome, he demanded that these Celtic Christians submit. They had followed their own tradition for centuries, so they were resistant to change. Furthermore, they were offended by the rudeness of Augustine, who even refused to stand when Celtic bishops paid him a visit. A cordial meeting of the minds would be decades away.

After Augustine died about 604, Roman missionaries pushed north across Britain, while Celtic missionaries under Columba were advancing south from Scotland. Both groups were converting Anglo-Saxons, and a collision seemed inevitable. The tension even reached the royal family because Oswy, king of most of the Anglo-Saxons, was influenced by the Celtic church, but his queen was from the south and thus was Roman in her beliefs.

In 664 Oswy convened a meeting to hear arguments from both sides. He would then determine which version of Christianity England would embrace. Dignified

Roman bishops and wild-looking Celtic believers met at Whitby. Some of the issues may seem silly today, but they weren't at the time. The two groups used different methods for deciding the date of Easter. Celtic monks wore a different tonsure (haircut) and could marry; Roman monks could not. Celtic bishops operated rather loosely under a monastery rather than under an archbishop, and the Celtic church did not recognize the authority of Rome's pope.

During the meeting before Oswy, the two groups appealed to different authorities: the Celts to Columba, the Romans to Peter. When Oswy asked the Celts if it was true, as the Romans said, that Christ gave the keys of heaven to Peter, they agreed. Oswy then decided in favor of the ones who could let him into paradise. Though some of the Celtic church resisted for generations, the future course of Christianity in England was set toward Rome.

The Church of England would evolve from this blend of Celtic and Roman traditions. While retaining some of its Celtic roots, especially its love of learning, it grew progressively more Roman Catholic in structure. The unique heritage of Celtic Christianity gradually faded, but it has enjoyed a resurgence of interest in modern times.

BEDE (672–735)

A Venerable Saint

Some believe that, before the Reformation, only the Roman Catholic and Eastern Orthodox churches descended from early Christianity. And indeed, these were the largest branches growing from Christian roots. But as we've seen, a third branch, independent of the other two, thrived on the British Isles: the Celtic church. Most of our knowledge of this third group comes from Bede, a Roman Catholic monk from northern Britain.

The details of Bede's life are shrouded in history, and the little we know comes from his own pen. When he was seven, his family gave him to Abbot Benedict Biscop to be raised and educated at the twin monasteries at Wearmouth and Jarrow. There he spent his life, studying Scripture, Latin, Greek, law, mathematics, and writing.

The intellectual life flourished within the Anglo-Saxon Christianity of Bede's age, and the monastery at Jarrow was especially known for its scholarship. Its library was well stocked with biblical manuscripts and the early fathers' commentaries on the Scriptures. Bede spent most of his time working with these manuscripts—the ideal background to prepare Jarrow's future master of education. He became a theologian and the greatest expert on the history of Christianity in England.

As an Anglo-Saxon Roman Catholic, Bede considered the Synod of Whitby to be the premier event in English Christian history. He supported its verdict and argued for Roman rather than Celtic ways. But he was fair-handed in praising the zeal of Celtic missionaries and the superior commitment of Ireland's saints and scholars compared to English Christians. Intentionally or not, his model was Eusebius, historian of the early church. Bede served the church in the eighth century by recording the history of God's people as Eusebius had four centuries before.

Bede wrote about forty works in Latin: biblical commentaries, grammars, science, and biographies of saints. His *Ecclesiastical History of the English People* is his most noted book and the main source of his legacy. He also popularized the calendar that divided history into BC and AD, before and after Christ. In crediting his sources and verifying facts rather than repeating legends, he was ahead of his time. Seven centuries later William Tyndale identified Augustine as his favorite early church expositor and Bede as his favorite medieval writer.

The monastic rule practiced at Jarrow was written by Biscop, its founder, but Bede knew the Rule of Benedict and followed it. His fellow monks so respected his life of devotion that soon after he died they referred to him as the Venerable Bede, and the title stuck. The most learned man of his age, he preserved the light of classical and patristic times. His effect on the scholarship of England and Europe would have been even greater had Vikings not destroyed his monastery in the next century. No one knows how much of his work was lost.

Few of us are monks or scholars, but Bede's saintly life models traits we can all aspire to. We may not pour our lives into ancient documents, but we can study Scripture, live humbly, and build a legacy that will positively affect those who follow in our footsteps.

Apostle to the Germans

For a thousand years, the Roman Empire ruled a large portion of the world. But in 410, after a steep decline in the empire's virtue and power, Alaric and his Visigoths sacked the city of Rome itself. The unthinkable had begun: The world's greatest empire would be no more. Finally, in 476, leaders from the invading Germanic tribes replaced the ruling line of Augustus. These semi-civilized people, who knew neither Greek nor Latin (and thus were "barbarians"), took control; their migration across the Rhine/Danube frontier was complete.

Most of these uninvited northerners were pagans; a few were Arians. Could such wild tribes be tamed, let alone be won to Christ? The church shuddered at the task; would it even survive these pillaging hordes? And worse, by the early seventh century, the Church of Rome was part of the problem as its own spiritual, moral, and intellectual virtue had faded.

But not all the church suffered spiritual disarray. Celtic believers in Ireland and Britain had been squeezed into the corners of their island world but had not been overrun. Their monasteries nurtured evangelistic zeal as well as scholarly passion, and they would soon send missionaries to northern Europe.

The most effective was Winfrid, later known by his Latin name: Boniface. He was born in Devonshire, England, but was a devoted follower of the Roman Church. In his early years he pursued the monastic way and excelled in his studies, eventually becoming a teacher, then a priest. In 716 he sailed for what is now Holland to evangelize the Frisians. But that work failed, and he went home to head a monastery in England. Three years later he hit the road again, first visiting Rome to win the pope's approval. Armed with papal authority, he set his sights on Germany, intending to bring it under Rome's rule.

Boniface's credibility with the pagans skyrocketed when (at least according to legend) he chopped down the sacred oak of Thor the thunder god before the horrified pagan worshipers. When Thor did not respond, reports spread about the superior power of the Christian God. Boniface and his English helpers converted the masses and established monasteries. In 732 the pope made him archbishop at large so he could organize the region fully under Rome's control. He worked in Germany most of his life but in 752 returned to Frisia, the place of his earlier failure. Two years later, as he prepared to baptize a group of converts, he was martyred by a pagan mob.

This "apostle to the Germans" has been called the greatest missionary of the Dark Ages, but he receives mixed reviews from non-Roman Catholics. He changed the religious face of Europe forever by steering it toward Roman Catholicism and away from paganism and Arianism. But because he thought Roman Catholocism was the only acceptable form of Christianity, he considered Celtic believers and other Christians to be false prophets. Furthermore, by enlisting the political support of the Carolingians in Gaul, he married church and state more closely than they already were.

Today Boniface is applauded for including women in his mission work, but his method of evangelizing by mass conversions is debated. His heart was fully devoted to Rome, and he expanded the Church's influence as did few others. Due in part to his efforts, most of Europe would be Roman Catholic until the sixteenth century.

How the West Was Won

The Western Roman Empire collapsed in the fifth century, but the Western church sustained its influence into the Middle Ages. The Eastern church, however, was threatened by an aggressive new religion: Islam. A conflict of worldviews was inevitable as the church struggled to survive Islam's expansion. But then an eighth-century battle would shape the face of Europe for centuries to come.

First, we need some historical background to set the stage. After the western half of the empire fell, the invading German tribes intermarried with the Romans and blended their cultures. By the end of the fifth century, France was occupied by one of these new Roman/German people groups, known as the Franks. Under the leadership of Clovis, the Franks united and rose to prominence. In 496 Clovis was converted to Christianity, thus preserving the church in Western Europe for the near future. The Franks grew weaker over the next two centuries, but a warrior named Charles of Heristal (Charlemagne's grandfather) rose to power in 714. He is

26 THE MEDIEVAL CHURCH UNITED (590–1054)

not widely known today, but he would play a major role in the history of Western Europe.

In the East, Muhammad was born about 570 near Mecca in Arabia. None could have suspected that this illiterate camel driver would become a religious reformer. But in 610 he had a vision that he interpreted as a call to preach monotheism—belief in one god. This was a radical change for the people of Arabia, who were polytheists—believers in many gods.

His preaching career began in Mecca with little success. But by 622 his followers became so numerous that the people of Mecca forced them to leave. In 630, after his movement had grown to thousands, they returned and captured Mecca. By the time Muhammad died two years later, his followers had subdued most of the Arabian peninsula and were looking for new worlds to conquer. In the next twenty years, Islam spread with dramatic speed across Syria, Palestine, Egypt, and Persia, including taking Jerusalem.

Islam's rapid expansion was due to several factors: the Muslims' fanatical enthusiasm for converting people; a belief that their religion and civilization were superior to all others; the use of military force to spread their faith; and the hope of plunder from their conquests. Opponents were forced to convert to Islam, pay tribute, or be killed. Within a century of Muhammad's death, Islam spread eastward to Pakistan and westward to Morocco. It eliminated the church in North Africa and eventually forced the Eastern church to live under Muslim political rule.

A Muslim army crossed the Strait of Gibraltar from Africa in 711 and conquered Spain in 718. It soon began raids through the Pyrenees Mountains along Spain's northern border and advanced into France. Their northern surge proceeded through France to Tours, only one hundred miles from Paris. There they met the forces of Charles of Heristal and were finally defeated. As a result of his victory, he became known as the Hammer, or Charles Martel in French.

Few today have heard of the Battle of Tours, but this relatively unknown event changed the world forever. Without this medieval military victory, Western Europe, and perhaps North America, might be Islamic today. God's use of otherwise ordinary people in obscure events can affect millions for centuries to come. We cannot imagine now how God will use us and the consequences of our decisions and actions on future generations.

The Giant King

Most Americans value the separation of church and state. None of us want the government telling us what to believe or not to believe. But during the Middle Ages, secular rulers, religious leaders, and common people throughout Europe thought church and state should be united in an empire of Christendom.

As leaders of Germanic and Frankish tribes converted to Christianity, they acquired authority in the church. At the same time, bishops were gaining political power as they filled the vacuum of leadership after the collapse of Rome. As the two trends continued, the distinction between political and religious power diminished.

The grandson of Charles Martel was a visionary and, a warrior, a natural leader always near the front of the hunt or battle, and a fine horseman, which was amazing because he was seven feet tall. His name was Charlemagne (Charles the Great). In 768 his father, Pepin III, divided his kingdom between Charles and his brother Carloman, but Carloman died in 771, leaving the Frankish Empire to Charles. His fifty campaigns doubled his father's territory, expanding his own realm in every direction until he ruled more of Europe than anyone since the fall of Rome.

A surprising opportunity arose in the spring of 799, when Pope Leo III was attacked and beaten by supporters of the previous pope. Leo was rescued, but he knew he needed more muscle for protection. So he appealed to Charles, who was happy to help. On Christmas Day 800, Charles was in Rome celebrating the holiday at St. Peter's Cathedral. As he prayed on bended knee, Pope Leo placed a golden crown on his head, announcing that he was the new Caesar. The Christian Roman Empire was born.

Charles was up to the task. He restored law and order after three centuries of chaos. And though he could barely read, he valued culture and learning. He gathered the finest thinkers to revive the intellectual life, which had suffered so much outside of Ireland. He recruited Alcuin (735–804), the great scholar from York in England, to be his headmaster.

Charles wanted to spark a renaissance of learning in Paris. The curriculum established by Alcuin attracted scholars and students to Paris for four hundred years, making it the intellectual center of Europe. In 1231 the pope recognized this consortium of scholars as the University of Paris.

When Charles died in 814, he left his empire to his son Louis. But neither Louis nor his successors possessed the strength or genius of Charlemagne, and within a hundred years any real sense of empire was gone. By the tenth century, the remains had split into France in the west and Germany-Austria in the east.

We can hardly overestimate Charlemagne's influence on Europe. In his wake, German rulers kept the dream of a revived Roman Empire alive until Napoleon finally crushed it in 1806. For a thousand years, Europe's politics and law, education and culture, were Christianized even though not always Christian. The Christian remnants in Europe today are a legacy to Charlemagne twelve hundred years after his coronation by the pope.

The Third Rome

For seventy years the vast Soviet Empire was ruled from the Kremlin. During that time, government oppression of religious people surpassed that of any other time in history. The Stalinist purges of the late 1930s were the pinnacle, wiping out millions of Orthodox, Baptists, and others. Finally, in 1991, the so-called workers' paradise collapsed, three years after the Russian Orthodox Church celebrated its millennial birthday. One can almost taste the happy irony.

Slavic believers hold to a fourth-century tradition that the apostle Andrew brought Christianity to the areas later known as Ukraine and Russia. Nothing truly historical, however, is known of the alleged Christian presence among the Slavic people before Viking Christians arrived and established a church in Kiev about 945.

The new faith was given a boost as Olga, widow of Prince Igor, became a Christian in 954. When her pagan grandson Vladimir came to the throne, he thought his people would benefit from adopting one of the major religions. He sent an envoy to investigate Judaism and Islam as well as Western and Eastern versions of Christianity. When his emissaries returned and described the options, he rejected Islam and Judaism because he didn't want to give up pork or be circumcised. He chose Eastern Orthodoxy over Roman Catholicism because Orthodox worship was pictured as so magnificent that it compared to heaven.

In 988 Vladimir renounced his pagan god and ordered the people of Kiev, the capital, to assemble on the banks of the Dnieper River to be baptized under his watchful eye. Refusal meant that you were an enemy of the state. The masses dutifully appeared and were baptized as one. Vladimir's son Yaroslav the Wise succeeded him in 1019 and accepted a bishop appointed by the patriarch of Constantinople. Thus the knot was formally tied with the Eastern Orthodox church.

But trouble was brewing over the eastern horizon. In the thirteenth century, Mongol horsemen appeared from nowhere and raced across Eastern Europe, plundering Kiev in 1237. Russian monks retreated to the northern forests just as the early Christians had fled for their spiritual lives to the deserts of Egypt and Syria. The forest monasteries preserved the arts and learning as Western monasteries had during their Dark Ages. In the south, Islam spread and increasingly threatened the

Eastern church, whose spiritual and political headquarters migrated north as the metropolitan of Kiev moved his headquarters to Moscow in 1328.

About the time when Islamic armies were conquering Constantinople in 1453, the Mongol grip on Moscow was relaxing. The mantle of Christian leadership fell from Constantinople's shoulders and landed on Moscow, considered the Third Rome by its religious leaders over the centuries. In 1547 Ivan IV called himself czar (a form of Caesar), and the Third Rome began building cathedrals, including one called the Kremlin.

The czars and the Orthodox Church guided the Russian people until the Bolshevik Revolution of 1917. For the following seventy years, even under mandatory atheism, tens of millions in the Soviet Union considered themselves Orthodox. Finally, after trying to exterminate religion for seven decades, the Soviet state crumbled. The church had endured atrocities and terror because faithful Orthodox and Baptist believers clung to their faith. Most of their heroic stories died with the martyrs, locked in heaven's memory to be released at a future date.

A Big Family Fight

Some people think of Roman Catholicism and Eastern Orthodoxy as twin sisters, with Protestantism as a distant cousin. That conclusion makes sense if we look only at external appearances. Next to the elaborate rituals and ceremonies of Catholicism and Orthodoxy, Protestantism is noticeably simple. But long before Protestantism was a gleam in the eye of Martin Luther, the two centers of medieval Christianity, Rome and Constantinople, had drifted apart. How did the "twin sisters" become so alienated?

From early in Christian history, two major differences were growing. The first was different levels of involvement in politics. In 330 Emperor Constantine moved his capital from Rome to Constantinople. Because the Eastern Church was headquartered in the new capital city, it now lived under the watchful eye of the emperor and thus avoided much involvement in politics. But when the Roman Empire fell, the Church of Rome assumed political power and even expanded it over time. Second, each held to different sources of authority. The

Church of Rome operated under the authority of the pope; the church in the East was guided by the seven great church councils. Given the passage of centuries, the intellectual and cultural divide had grown into an impassable gulf.

Within that broad context, particular issues developed, including different rituals and types of bread in Communion, different days for fasting and the date of Easter, and disagreement over clergy marriage and the use of icons. But the big spark was the Western insertion of a clause into the Nicene Creed affirming that the Spirit proceeded from the Son as well as from the Father. Who was the Church in Rome, Eastern Christians argued, to change the Nicene Creed? Eastern theologians smelled heresy—tampering with the Trinity.

The pot began to boil in the eleventh century when Norman Vikings invaded southern Italy and forced the Greeks who lived there to abandon their Eastern church practices and follow the Roman Church. The patriarch of Constantinople responded by demanding that Western churches near him comply with Greek practices. They refused; he shut them down.

The big blowup of 1054 was sparked by a visit to Constantinople from a Roman delegation led by Cardinal Humbert. They entered the cathedral of St.

Sophia and placed on the altar a letter of excommunication. Anticipating its contents, a deacon grabbed the document and chased after the Roman delegation as they left. He tried unsuccessfully to force it into their hands, and as it fell to the street, all hope of unity disappeared.

The pope of the West had excommunicated Patriarch Cerularius and the whole Eastern church. Not to be outdone, Cerularius excommunicated the whole Western church a week later. Almost every Christian in the world was excommunicated. That may strike us as laughable, but it wasn't funny then. Most people thought calmer diplomats could soon fix the mess and reinstate the faithful on both sides. Negotiations continued, but no formal reconciliation was achieved.

Forty years later, the growing and militant religion of Islam was threatening the Eastern Orthodox Church. They asked Rome for help, and the pope responded by sending Crusaders to fight the advancing Islamic armies. But in 1182 old tensions led to anti-Roman riots in Constantinople. Finally, in 1204, Crusaders from Rome destroyed all hope of reconciliation by pillaging Constantinople. The Eastern church has not yet forgotten those three days of unrestrained horror, and the two churches remain divorced.

Mind and Heart as One

By the eleventh century, the Roman Church and its monasteries had grown immoral and corrupt, in part due to political meddling. So Western Europe debated the question of who should control the church and appoint its officials: the king or the pope? A reform movement to clean up the monasteries had begun at Cluny in France, and as it spread, the desire to free the church from the king gained popularity.

In 1075 Pope Gregory VII issued a decree that no laypeople, kings, or others could choose the clergy and that secular rulers must submit to him, the pope. William the Conqueror from Normandy agreed, and after he captured England, the reforms were applied there. Ironically, when he died in 1093, his successor, King William II, appointed the new archbishop of Canterbury, a monk named Anselm.

Anselm was born in 1033 to a noble family at Aosta in the mountains of northern Italy. His pious mother influenced him toward the things of God, so as a youth he studied with Benedictine monks. At age twenty-three

30 THE MEDIEVAL CHURCH DIVIDED (1054–1517)

he left home for formal training under the famed scholar Lanfranc at the monastery of Bec in Normandy, France, where he would spend thirty years of his life.

Anselm became a monk at age twenty-seven and prior of the monastery three years later. His fame as a thinker and writer spread, and in 1078 he was forced to succeed Lanfranc as abbot. He agreed with the reformers, so he resisted when King William II appointed him archbishop of Canterbury in 1093. But the pope wanted Anselm in that position, and because of his monastic vows of obedience, he complied with the pope's wishes. During his career, he continued to resist the orders of English kings, resulting in two exiles.

Anselm lived during a time of exceptional scholarship, when the church produced great thinkers and supervised all education. Drawing on the ancient Greek philosophies of Aristotle, Plato, and Socrates, Anselm and other scholars organized their theology from the Bible and early church fathers, especially Augustine. Anselm's many writings reveal his uncommon mind. They record his ontological argument for the existence of God (an effort by logic alone to prove God's existence), which is still debated among philosophers and theologians.

He did not, however, throw out faith in his use of reason to search for truth. Like Augustine, Anselm believed that faith is the first step toward understanding, not the other way around. In addition to his works on philosophy and theology, he wrote prayers and meditations to help monks and laypeople achieve deeper spiritual vitality. His popular devotional guides sharpened the attention and focused the mind and heart on God.

Anselm was a skilled church administrator, but his legacy was his ability to solve intellectual problems. Even on his deathbed, he wanted more time to wrestle with the question of the origin of the human soul. One of the intellectual giants of the early second millennium, he helped set a new direction in Christian thinking.

In our day the mind and the heart are often divorced. By contrast, Anselm understood what many people, Christians as well as non-Christians, have forgotten: that loving God and loving ideas are not incompatible. Thinking, and thinking well, is a Christian activity.

For the Love of God

The father of medieval mysticism was born in 1090 near Dijon, France, the third of seven children from a knight and a noble lady. Probably because of his godly mother's influence, he chose the life of a monk instead of pursuing the training that fit his station in life.

After a year of preparation, Bernard began his monastic career at age twenty-one. But instead of joining an established monastery, he entered the new, reform-minded abbey of Cîteaux, France. Even then he displayed amazing leadership, taking thirty relatives with him into the cloistered life. Bernard's spiritual depth was so admired that in just four years the abbot asked him to start a new monastery in the remote valley of Clairvaux, where he served for the rest of his life.

Bernard's résumé shows a broad range of achievements. While abbot of Clairvaux, he founded sixty-five other monasteries and helped start three hundred more. In 1130 he was asked to mediate between Anacletus II and Innocent II, both of whom claimed to be the legitimate pope. (Innocent won partly due to Bernard's support.) In 1147 he was commissioned by Pope Eugenius III to preach across France and Germany for a second crusade. He agreed, perhaps out of loyalty to his father, who had been a knight in the first crusade (1096–1099).

Bernard detected heresy in Professor Peter Abelard's moral influence theory of the atonement. Christ's death was not a payment to appease God's wrath against sin, Abelard taught, but a mere example of God's love, motivating us to love Him in return. Bernard's concern was validated in 1140 when the Council of Sens condemned Abelard.

In the midst of his other activities, Bernard wrote much theology as well as numerous personal letters (we have more than five hundred of them). He pictured the stages of spiritual development as degrees of love for God. Consistent with that theme, he wrote that the purpose of study and meditation on Scripture is not to gather information but to reform the fallen divine image within and thus draw us closer to God. He did not teach a pantheistic merger with God's nature, as some later monks did, but rather a unity of our will and God's.

The ascetic rule he followed freed him from worldly concerns so he could live fully for God. But it was so severe that it damaged his health. Decades of harsh self-denial eventually overcame his body, and he died at Clairvaux in 1153. Only twenty-one years later, the Roman Church canonized him, and within a century writers were referring to him as one of the church fathers. Dante's *Divine Comedy*, written in the early 1300s, shows Bernard not just in Paradise but in God's presence. The great mystic monk had made his mark.

Both sides in the Reformation claimed him as theirs: Luther and Calvin considered him a forerunner of their own work. They were especially impressed by his writing on justification and Christ's saving work, reflecting Bernard's lifelong immersion in the Bible.

The most powerful person of the twelfth century, Bernard founded monasteries, refereed between competing popes, preached a crusade, opposed heretics, and wrote love poems to God. His legacy connects two ages: the old feudal era of knights and ladies and the new era of cities and universities. Most of all, Bernard loved God with a passion seldom found today.

A Gathering of Scholars

Today, people tend to think of a university in two ways: as the place where high school grads go for a good time, and as the home of their favorite football team. Thinking of a university as an arena for serious study and intellectual exploration rates a distant third, if it rates at all.

Universities, as we know them, started in the twelfth century when the recovery of Aristotle's writings set Europe on a new path. The question: Could philosophy (logic) and theology coexist in a unified whole? The new frontier for medieval scholars was how to mix faith and reason.

Integrating the world of ideas with the doctrines of the church sparked the genius of great thinkers. These men and their disciples loved ideas and how they fit together. Some of the well-known scholastics, or schoolmen, from the ninth to the fourteenth centuries were Anselm, Peter Abelard, Peter Lombard, and Thomas Aquinas. They took seriously the words of Jesus and Paul: "Love the Lord your God . . . with all your *mind*" and "Be transformed by the renewing of your *mind*" (Matthew 22:37 and Romans 12:2, emphasis added).

Centers of learning emerged as students gathered to hear their favorite teachers lecture. Like medieval craftsmen, scholars formed guilds to guard their profession. They referred to themselves as a "university," which at the time meant any association or group of people. They first met in cathedrals, town squares, or rented rooms, and if the place proved inconvenient or the locals unreceptive, they simply moved on. Professors charged a fee for their reading and commentary on a text. Students paid after each day's class—an early form of tuition. In effect, they hired their professor.

Latin was required to enter a university, which students did at age sixteen to eighteen, although an exceptional student might be accepted as early as fourteen. Only teachers had textbooks, so memorization was essential to survive the academic regimen. Teaching methods centered on lecture and debate. Competing masters argued the fine points of logic on the issues of the day before their cheering students, and young minds began to turn for themselves, developing skills of critical analysis and independent thinking.

The four- to six-year curriculum leading to a bachelor's degree was built around the liberal arts: grammar, rhetoric, arithmetic, geometry, astronomy, music, and logic (philosophy). Two more years of study, a teaching assistantship, and a thesis led to a master's degree in law, medicine, or theology. At Paris (the top university of the time), six years beyond the master's resulted in a doctor of divinity degree, and three to six more years were needed for the ultimate doctor of sacred theology degree. Today's programs seem diluted by comparison.

Most of Europe's great universities began during this time. By 1400, more than seventy-five dotted the continent. Universities grew in prestige as well as numbers and changed the world in two ways: by helping to secularize society, and by helping to lead to the Reformation. Two of the greatest pre-Reformers were theology professors in the university system: John Wycliffe at Oxford and Jan Hus at Prague. Martin Luther was later a professor of theology at the University of Wittenberg.

The university idea arose from the desire to integrate faith and reason, but over time most universities abandoned faith for reason alone. That change was the main influence in secularizing Western culture. But a few courageous voices today, such as historian George Marsden and the MacLaurin Institute at the University of Minnesota, are resurrecting the original idea of faith integrated with reason in the pursuit of truth. A renaissance of intellectual integrity is beginning.

The Dumb Ox

Intellectual challenges can threaten or strengthen faith as we think more deeply about our beliefs and how they fit our world. In the thirteenth century, the church faced that challenge as Jewish and Islamic commentaries on Aristotle's writings arrived in European universities.

Thomas Aquinas was born for such a time. The son of a count and countess and related to royalty, he grew up in a castle near Naples, Italy. His first teachers, Benedictine monks at Monte Cassino, convinced his parents to send him at age fourteen to the University of Naples, where he soon excelled. From there he traveled to Paris to study under famed tutor Albert the Great.

Aquinas was quiet, serious, and heavy, earning from classmates the nickname Dumb Ox. His size may have compared to that of an ox, but he was anything but dumb. He eventually received the necessary degrees to teach theology, and he traveled from university to university as the church's most celebrated defender against the encroaching secularism.

THE MEDIEVAL CHURCH
DIVIDED (1054–1517) | **33**

The central concern was not Aristotle but the interplay of faith and reason that resulted from Aristotle's insights. Could a person of faith maintain that faith in the light of reason's new discoveries? Aquinas pursued a middle path, not selling out to Aristotle's ideas, as some theologians had, but still accepting what was true from the ancient sage.

Aquinas believed in what theologians call *general revelation* within nature and ourselves—basic truths such as God's existence and power. More detailed ideas, such as the Incarnation and the Trinity, were taught through *special revelation*—Jesus Christ and Scripture. Because God's truth revealed by either method cannot contradict itself, it could be synthesized, which Aquinas tried to do. He did not replace faith with reason but instead applied reason to help faith understand God and His truth.

Aquinas's literary output matched the enormous range of his thoughts. Eighteen massive volumes contain sermons, commentaries on the Bible and on Peter Lombard's *Sentences*, and dialogues with Aristotle. They also include his two most profound works: *Summa theologiae*, his summary of Christian belief about everything (which he never finished), and *Summa contra Gentiles*, his arguments defending the faith.

Aquinas could think faster than he could write (and no one could read his handwriting anyway), so he dictated multiple subjects to several secretaries simultaneously. He wrote for his classroom, and his work was used throughout the Middle Ages as the standard theology text. During the Reformation, both sides mined his religious ideas for support.

After a supernatural experience in 1273, he ended his writing career, explaining that compared to what he had seen, all he had written was merely straw. Three months later, at the age of forty-nine, he died. The Roman Catholic Church used his works at the Council of Trent (1545–1563) as the basis for its decrees, and in 1879 Pope Leo XIII proclaimed Aquinas's works valid forever. He is considered the greatest Roman Catholic theologian between Augustine and the current day, but the Reformers also appealed to him as an authority to argue their views.

The Dumb Ox is now called the Angelic Doctor. Much of his life was spent reading or writing books. Today Catholics and Protestants alike benefit from his devotion to truth. From Aquinas we learn to grapple with the intellectual challenges of the day without giving in or running away. Ideas are tools for the glory of God, and God gave each of us a mind to use in His service.

THE WALDENSIANS
(TWELFTH CENTURY–PRESENT)

Where's Waldo?

Children love to search a picture full of people and play *Where's Waldo*? Even the funny name Waldo brings a smile. But the name has a noble heritage in church history, referring to Waldo of Lyons in southern France. Despite terrible odds, the small band of devoted Christians known as Waldensians survived and gave us a remarkable example of faith under persecution.

About 1170 a wealthy merchant named Peter Valdes (Waldo's Latin name) decided to obey, in a literal sense, Jesus' words "If you want to be perfect, go, sell your possessions and give to the poor, and you will have treasure in heaven. Then come, follow me" (Matthew 19:21). Waldo paid for someone to translate part of the Bible into the language of the people, then gave his wealth to the poor so he could live in poverty and preach the gospel as the apostles had.

Waldo attracted a following of common, uneducated people who wanted to live the simple life and preach the gospel. Such sacrifice was not unknown at the time, but it had to be sanctioned by the Church. The final decision bounced between pope and archbishop before the verdict came: No untrained people could preach. The Waldensians had no desire to threaten the Church or start a new one, but because they refused to comply with the Church's prohibition against preaching the gospel, they were excommunicated.

Waldensian beliefs anticipated issues that ignited the Reformation in the sixteenth century. They believed in the Bible's authority and wanted it translated into the common language. They emphasized individual Bible study, personal commitment to following Christ, and a passion for evangelism. They also rejected Roman doctrines of purgatory, praying to saints, the intercession of priests, and most of the seven sacraments. The issue that created the most tension with Rome was their conviction that anyone could preach and teach the Bible; in their view, one didn't have to be a priest or a monk—or be formally trained at all.

But Rome wasn't about to share its authority to dispense God's truth, especially with untrained laypeople. The clash of wills escalated in 1184 when the Waldensians were excommunicated by the Council of Verona. Over the centuries they were the targets of the Inquisition, and thousands were massacred as a result of papal decree. Many fled to the Alps along the borders of France, Italy, and Switzerland. Others spread across the continent, mostly to central and eastern Europe.

The Waldensians encountered other pre-Protestant groups, such as followers of Jan Hus in Bohemia and John Wycliffe in England. Some Waldensian doctrines matched those of the great Reformers of the sixteenth century, but others varied, including the doctrine of salvation. Nevertheless, many of their views became mainstream during the Reformation, and in 1532 they adopted a confession of faith that marked them as a Protestant group. In the early nineteenth century, some Waldensians emigrated to Uruguay, Argentina, and the United States. (About twenty thousand exist today.)

The Waldensians' commitment to Scripture and to following Christ in the midst of persecution rivals that of any group in history. They have been called the oldest evangelical church, and we may draw courage from their example.

The Morning Star of the Reformation

Fourteenth-century Oxford scholar John Wycliffe loved the Bible. But the only Bible available at the time was in Latin. As a medieval scholar, Wycliffe knew Latin. Yet as a zealot for God's Word, he dreamed of an English Bible readable by the common people.

Wycliffe's early years are largely unknown. He was born in Lutterworth in northern England about 1330. He spent most of his life as the leading theologian and philosopher at Oxford, Europe's greatest university in the fourteenth century.

Wycliffe anticipated doctrines made famous by Martin Luther 150 years later.

- Christ, not the pope, is the head of the church.
- The priest's main job is to preach the Bible, not be a Church-appointed mediator between people and God.

- One's individual relationship with God, not the Church's religious system, is of supreme importance.
- Christ's work, rather than our own, gained God's merit.

Perhaps his most radical belief was that Scripture, not the Church, is the authority for truth and life. Wycliffe believed that people could not know the Christian faith without knowing the Bible, and they would know the Bible best if they could study it in their own language. So he and his friends translated the Latin Bible into the English of the ordinary people.

Wycliffe's belief in a Bible for everyone, along with his dynamic preaching and teaching, attracted both a following and opposition from the highest level: the pope condemned his views in 1377. Within a few years, his support at Oxford declined, and his voice was increasingly silenced at the school he helped to make great. Eventually, the Roman Church and some of his Oxford colleagues forced him from the university because of his radical views. But his removal did not stop his writing, and he continued to send his followers into the countryside and the churches with a few pages of the translated Bible to preach to farmers and merchants. Their effectiveness across England threatened the Roman Church, so in 1401 the Church pushed a bill through Parliament, making it a crime to preach Wycliffe's ideas, punishable by death.

Wycliffe spent his last years in his home church at Lutterworth, where he died of a stroke while leading worship on New Year's Eve 1384. Even after his death, the Roman Church still opposed him. At the Council of Constance, thirty-one years later, he was condemned for heresy and excommunicated. Then, in 1428, the Roman Church dug up Wycliffe's bones, burned them, and spread the ashes in a nearby river, hoping to rid the world of his memory and influence.

Wycliffe's impact is seen in the main charge brought against Martin Luther—that of renewing Wycliffe's insistence of making Scripture the authority over the Church. To this day, Wycliffe is known as the Morning Star of the Reformation. His name is memorialized by the Wycliffe Bible Translators, who carry on his passion for translating the Bible into the common languages of people around the world.

God's truth will not be buried even by determined opposition. As we learn it, live it, and courageously proclaim it, God will use it in the lives of people who see and hear us.

JAN HUS (C. 1369–1415)

Give Me Truth or Give Me Death

Actions count for more than words, and martyrdom makes the words ring true forever. Church history records many martyrs, some killed by the church itself. One of them was Jan Hus, born to peasant parents in Husinec, Bohemia, in today's Czech Republic.

Hus acquired his bachelor's and master's degrees in theology at the University of Prague, a bastion of growing nationalism among the Czech people. Because he had been an excellent student and was known for his godly character, he was hired after graduation to fill a teaching post at that university. He may not have been an original thinker like Wycliffe a generation before, but his Czech students loved his lectures.

In 1400 Hus was ordained a priest and appointed to the Bethlehem Church in Prague. Then in 1402 he was promoted to become rector of the university. From pulpit and lectern, the charismatic Hus changed the world by popularizing Wycliffe's radical ideas, which he had learned as a student. But Church authorities were listening.

Hus promoted Wycliffe's belief that everyone should be able to read the Bible in his or her native tongue. He incorporated Wycliffe's ideas in his own sermons and writings, implanting a passion for God's Word and setting ablaze the hearts of his students and parishioners. Because Wycliffe had been condemned as a heretic, Hus was forbidden by both popes (there were two at the time) from preaching and teaching his ideas, but the fiery rebel refused to stop.

A public figure like Hus couldn't snub Rome without making powerful enemies. He believed that Christ, not the pope, was the head of the Church. Doctrines not found in the Bible weren't true, even if Roman clergy said they were, and Hus refused to teach them. News of his defiance raced across Europe. He had called Rome's bluff. A showdown was inescapable when he was summoned to the city of Constance to defend his words before Church authorities.

Safe passage was guaranteed, but once he was there, the promise was revoked because the Church didn't need to keep its word to a "heretic." He was imprisoned for eight months, and on July 6, 1415, he was condemned and sentenced to be burned at the stake. When given a final chance to recant before the fire was lit, his last words were that he would gladly die for the truth of the gospel.

Hus's martyrdom propelled his followers into even greater pre-Protestant fervor, tilling the soil that Luther would work into a harvest called the Reformation. Hus loyalists formed the Bohemian Brethren, which developed into the Moravian Church, a missionary-minded group that influenced John Wesley in the eighteenth century.

One might think that leaders in Rome would have learned from their miscalculation, but they repeated it almost exactly with Luther a century later. He followed in Hus's footsteps, accusing the Church of the same errors and setting Europe ablaze with more "heretical" ideas. So close were the similarities that Luther was called "the Saxon Hus."

Today, Jan Hus is celebrated as a Czech hero who refused to say the words that would have spared his life. In 1999 the Roman Catholic Church finally apologized for what they had done to Hus five hundred years before. May the church of Christ have more heroes like Hus, whose fidelity to the truth was more important than saving his skin.

The Death of the Second Rome

After September 11, 2001, people asked how anyone could kill innocent people in the name of religion. But that wasn't the first time that zealots, from any religion, have murdered in the name of God. When a jihad is proclaimed, faithful Muslims are compelled to join. The basic meaning of the word *jihad* is "struggle," but it has come to mean "holy war." A jihad may be of the heart, mouth, hand, or sword. That fourth form is literal and glorious to many militant Muslims.

One of the greatest victories of the Islamic sword was the fall of Constantinople, capitol of the Byzantine Empire. The Byzantine Empire comprised the eastern half of the Roman Empire after Rome fell and Greek ways became dominant in the East. Perhaps remembering the sack of Rome, defenders built great walls to protect this "second Rome." As the city lay safe within, Islamic civilization overpowered much of the region, sometimes by ideas, often by the sword.

THE MEDIEVAL CHURCH DIVIDED (1054–1517) | **37**

In the late fourteenth century, the Balkans fell to a new Islamic force, the Ottoman Turks. Their rule spread across southeastern Europe in the direction of Constantinople. (Today's struggle between Muslims and Orthodox Christians in that region dates back to this period.) In April of 1453 the Turks under Sultan Mehmed II surrounded Constantinople with a hundred thousand men. With only ten thousand defenders, the well-fortified city withstood the siege for fifty days as Turk cannons bombarded the walls and warships sealed the city from the sea. The infantry waited nearby to devour its prey.

Finally, in the middle of a night in May, the walls were breached. The first assault was repelled after two hours of fighting, but a second attack soon followed and gained entrance into the city. The defending Christians fought gallantly and killed most of the invaders by sunrise. Before the Christian army could regroup, though, a third assault was launched by the most elite Turk troops. Fierce hand-to-hand combat wore down the Christian defenders, but they still prevented the Turks from overrunning the city. Turk commanders called for reinforcements from their ships in the harbor. These disembarked and joined troops on the ground. The combined force was too much for the outnumbered and exhausted defenders. The city walls were completely breached and the pillaging began.

The eastern half of the Roman Empire outlived its western counterpart by a thousand years. But the second Rome was now in the hands of Islam and was renamed Istanbul. The Church of Hagia Sophia ("Holy Wisdom"), seat of the patriarch of Eastern Orthodoxy, was converted into a mosque. For the first time since the Battle of Tours in 732, Islamic armies were in a position to seriously threaten Europe. They twice forged their way west as far as Vienna but were defeated both times. After that they set their sights elsewhere until recent times.

Militant Muslims see modern terrorism as a continuation of the centuries-old Islamic war of conquest. Other religions have, from time to time, relied on force to defend themselves, but jihad lies at the core of the dreams held by extremist Muslims. May God give the world wisdom, strength, and endurance to deal with this resurgence of an old and serious threat.

The Birth of the Information Age

Everyone reading this book probably owns a Bible. We might therefore assume it has always been the case that every person has had a written copy of Scripture. But for three thousand years after Moses first wrote part of God's Word, few people owned a Bible.

Through all those centuries, scribes and monks hand-copied the Bible from previous copies. Mass-produced Bibles were unthinkable because no means to reproduce them existed other than rewriting the whole thing by hand. Copying books took time and cost money, so only the wealthy could buy them. That changed when a German printer named Johannes Gutenberg invented the printing press.

Gutenberg was not a monk or a theologian, but a businessman. Born as Hans Gensfleisch in Mainz, Germany, about 1398, he took the name Gutenberg after his father's estate. As a child, he was exposed to goldsmithing because his father worked for the local mint run by the archbishop. Gutenberg applied that metalworking craft to the printing business, experimenting with new methods. Like most inventions, the printing press didn't appear overnight, and Gutenberg risked everything he had, borrowing money to fund his innovative project.

His main assets were patience, determination, and the good sense to keep his invention secret before he perfected it. The breakthrough was not printing but movable type, so that letters could be rearranged and words reproduced quickly and easily. He designed a mold that could hold precisely shaped and sized pieces of wood, on which he made uniform metal letters.

After Gutenberg printed the Bible in 1454, presses soon appeared in Rome, Paris, and Westminster. By 1480, more than one hundred towns in Europe boasted a press, and over two hundred had one by 1500. More books were printed in a few years after Gutenberg than in many centuries before. The impact was explosive.

Ideas were now accessible to all, and revolutionary thoughts from the Renaissance and soon the Reformation raced across the European continent. Everyone could own a Bible, and people had a reason to learn to read. For the first time, the life of the mind was accessible to the ordinary person. Knowledge was com-

THE MEDIEVAL CHURCH DIVIDED (1054–1517) | **38**

mon property, no longer monopolized by the priests and the rich. When followers of Martin Luther printed his incendiary views, the world was set ablaze. Reformation doctrines flooded Europe within weeks of their birth and changed the world forever.

Our modern age would not have come about without books and the ideas they bear. The printing press paved the way for new political notions, such as individual liberty. Thoughts that led to the American government spread among the people through books and pamphlets. Only since Gutenberg has God's Word reached millions in written form. God's people have always been known as people of the Book, and thanks to Gutenberg, we can all have a copy of that Book. We should treasure it and thank God for it.

ERASMUS (C. 1468–1536)

Laying Luther's Egg

Fortunate are the churches whose pastors know New Testament Greek and use that knowledge to inform their preaching. The linguistic nuances and cultural context of the original wording shed marvelous light on the teachings of Jesus and the apostles—light that can go on illuminating lives long after Sunday morning. This privilege of receiving insights into the original language, however, is one that Christians have not always enjoyed. We owe a debt of gratitude for this change to Desiderius Erasmus of Rotterdam.

If any doubt remained that reformation was coming after Wycliffe and Hus, it became inevitable with Erasmus. A freethinker and profound scholar, he placed in Luther's heart the spark that ignited the Reformation. Or as others say, "Erasmus laid the egg that Luther hatched."

Erasmus was the illegitimate son of a Dutch priest. After the death of his parents when he was nine, he was sent to a school run by the Brethren of the Common Life, from whom he began receiving his classical training. In time he grudgingly became an Augustinian monk and was ordained a priest at age twenty-three in the year Columbus found the New World. But Erasmus hated monastic life with its "narrow" theologians and rigid rules, so he hit the road for the universities of Europe. There he was influenced most by the writings of Jerome, the early church scholar and translator who loved both the classics and the Bible.

Like other classical scholars, Erasmus was a man of ideas, and he believed that the Church should be reformed according to standards in Scripture. His big splash came from compiling the Greek New Testament. For a thousand years, the Church of Rome had used the Vulgate, Jerome's Latin translation. So where did Erasmus get this notion of resurrecting the Greek New Testament?

When Constantinople fell in 1453, scholars fled to the West, taking their Greek manuscripts with them. Erasmus knew that theology depended on the grammar of the biblical text in its original language. Without studying a Greek Testament, one's doctrine was suspect. Therefore, from the newly arrived, partial Greek manuscripts, he assembled the first complete Greek New Testament of "modern" times.

He had it printed so that every scholar could have a

copy to compare current Church beliefs with the original text. They discovered that the Church of Rome had drifted away from the apostolic age. The bomb found its way into Luther's hand and the fuse was lit. All of Europe soon felt the explosion. At first Erasmus supported Luther, but Luther's revolutionary ideas proved too much for the Dutch scholar, and he backed away from Luther's work.

In the preface of his Greek New Testament, Erasmus argued for translation of the Bible into the common languages of the day. In 1522 Luther did just that, translating Scripture into German. William Tyndale did the same, into English, in 1525. Other languages soon followed.

Pastors (and even laypeople) who want to know and teach the Bible well are wise to prepare in the original languages. Nothing compares to the inspired text studied, taught, and applied with depth. Serious, systematic study of Scripture in the original languages leads to a soul saturated with God's Word.

MARTIN LUTHER (1483–1546)

The Wild Boar

Luther was born on November 10, 1483, in Eisleben, Germany. His father's mining business generated enough profits to pay for a good education. Martin wasn't the brightest student, however, placing thirtieth out of fifty-seven on his pre-university exams. But he knew how to study, and he finished his bachelor's and master's degrees at the respected University of Erfurt in the minimum time allowed. His father hoped Martin would go into law, but when Martin was nearly struck by lightning during a thunderstorm, he promised St. Anne, patron saint of miners, that he would become a monk. He kept his word and joined an Augustinian monastery.

Even though Luther earned a doctorate in theology and was appointed professor at the University of Wittenberg, he was overwhelmed by his own sinfulness. He knew of God's wrath but not of His love. A pilgrimage to Rome in 1510 only intensified his longing to be free from guilt. As he prepared to teach Romans, he wrestled with how a righteous God could also be gracious, and

40 THE REFORMATION BEGINS (1517–1563)

he pored over Paul's words in 1:17, "The righteous will live by faith." Finally, he got it: The just live by God's righteousness, given to us by faith in Christ, rather than by our own good deeds. The doctrine of justification by faith was recovered—and Luther's tormented soul was reborn—the Reformation had begun.

Not one to keep his mouth shut, Luther posted ninety-five theses, or statements of belief, on the door of the Roman Catholic church at Wittenberg—a public forum. With the aid of the newly invented printing press, his revolutionary views were reproduced and rapidly spread across Europe. The pope responded by sending a papal bull (formal document) condemning forty-one of Luther's beliefs as heretical and calling him a wild boar in God's vineyard.

Luther's students responded by burning books of Church law. For good measure, Luther threw the pope's letter onto the fire. As theological salvos were traded between Rome and Wittenberg, Luther sharpened his arguments and expanded his doctrines, stressing that Scripture alone is the standard for truth and life. Rome knew that Luther's teaching could be a deathblow, so the pope excommunicated him for heresy and ordered him to appear for trial in the city of Worms (see essay 41).

German peasants ran wild with Luther's ideas and demanded a new social order. In 1525 they revolted—an action Luther condemned. He wanted to find the truth, not start an insurrection. One social change he did support was the right of clergy to marry, which he himself did. His wife, Katharina, a former nun, bore six children whom he loved dearly. He remained professor of theology at Wittenberg for the rest of his life. But his many trials and travels damaged his health, and at age sixty-two he died of a heart attack in Eisleben, the town of his birth.

The Roman Church had ruled Europe unhindered for a thousand years despite occasional challenges from the likes of Wycliffe, Hus, and the Waldensians. By exposing Rome's corruption and wayward theology, Luther broke its stranglehold on human souls. And for this accomplishment some call Luther the most important person of the second millennium. He never wanted to stir up trouble or split the Church, yet he changed the world. He just wanted to know God and to honor Him. Luther was a sometimes gruff but always humble man. He saw himself as a simple monk and teacher who wanted to know, live, and teach God's truth.

A Diet of Worms?

Few things sound less appealing than a diet of worms. This Diet, however, was not a dinner but a sixteenth-century council called by Charles V, emperor of the Holy Roman Empire. The purpose was to explore the "heretical" writings of Martin Luther, an obscure monk who taught theology at the University of Wittenberg.

Luther spent much of 1518 to 1520 debating other Roman Catholic scholars about issues surrounding the authority of the pope and the Church. In 1520 alone he published five books and many smaller works, all of which disagreed with the Church. Pope Leo X finally had enough, and in June of that year he issued a bull, or written mandate, condemning Luther. When Luther's books were burned, he responded by burning Leo's bull. In January 1521, Leo declared Luther a heretic and excommunicated him. Because the emperor was responsible to defend the Church and the empire from heresy, he ordered Luther to his council in the city of Worms to justify his radical writings.

The Diet met from January 27 to May 25, 1521,

with Luther appearing on April 17 and 18. The proceedings were conducted by the pope's representative, who ordered Luther to recant his "heresies." Luther refused unless someone could reveal his error by the testimony of Scripture and sound reason. He even offered to burn his own books if anyone could show that they violated Scripture. After being repeatedly pressed for a confession of heresy, he replied, "My conscience is captive to the Word of God. Thus I cannot and will not recant, for going against conscience is neither safe nor right. I can do no other, here I stand, God help me."

Luther was given twenty-one days of freedom before his sentence would be carried out, and he left the council on April 26. The emperor proclaimed Luther an outlaw, calling him "a devil in a monk's habit." Anyone in the empire was authorized to capture him and turn him over to the authorities, which would result in his death. Even reading his books was declared a crime. As Luther was returning to Wittenberg, his friends, under the direction of Frederick the Wise, prince of Saxony, kidnapped him and took him to Wartburg Castle. He spent the next year translating the New Testament from Latin into German so the common people could read it.

The underlying issue at the Diet of Worms was authority: Who was in charge—the Church of Rome or the Word of God? Luther proclaimed the authority of God's Word and thus challenged the Church's religious authority as well as its political influence over the subjects of the empire. The everyday practice of Christianity by common Christians also changed. Individual conscience, informed by Scripture, was held in higher regard than the dictates of ecclesiastical powers. Luther's courageous stand laid the foundation of the Protestant movement that had been a gleam in the eyes of Wycliffe and Hus.

One person's courage can change the world.

Chaplain Reformer

Today we think of Switzerland as a peaceful country, untouched by conflict and neutral in war. But in the early sixteenth century, the confederation of Swiss cantons (territories) provided mercenaries for the nations of Europe as well as the pope. Swiss Reformer Ulrich Zwingli opposed this practice, even though he served as chaplain to Swiss troops.

On New Year's Day 1484, the mayor of a village near Zürich welcomed the birth of his son, Ulrich. A mayor's salary could pay for a good education, so young Zwingli studied at Vienna, then finished his bachelor's and master's degrees at Basel in 1504 and 1506. Following his hero, Erasmus, he pursued studies in the humanities and languages, including Greek and Hebrew. Theology was not his favorite field.

After he was called as priest to Zürich, Zwingli worked with civic officials to rid the city of Roman Catholic images. His ideas weren't posted on the church door like Luther's but instead were delivered from the pulpit. Someone remarked that all that was left of the

42 THE REFORMATION BEGINS (1517–1563)

Swiss church was four walls and a sermon.

He loved the Greek New Testament, which he hand-copied from a copy of Erasmus's work. He memorized the letters of Paul in Greek and taught straight through books of the Bible. The impact of God's Word, explained and applied verse by verse, was explosive. His preaching was so popular that city officials ordered all preaching to be based on Scripture.

But new ideas and biblical preaching often lead to conflict. Even the Reformers disagreed on some issues, including Luther and Zwingli on the meaning of Communion. So in 1529 they met at Marburg Castle in southwestern Germany to talk through their redis-covered doctrines. They agreed on fourteen of fifteen topics but not on Communion. Luther thought that a real, physical presence of Christ was somehow found in the elements; Zwingli believed the elements were only symbolic.

In October 1531 tensions arose over the evangeli-cal preaching in Zürich. Roman Catholic authorities in nearby cantons declared war on the city, which assem-bled a hasty defense. In the ensuing battle of Kappel, five hundred people from Zürich were killed, including Zwingli, chaplain of the troops. An enemy unit found him badly wounded, but before they finished him off, he was heard to say, "They can kill the body but not the soul."

Luther never wrote a systematic theology. The task of organizing Reformation doctrines fell to others, especially Zwingli and Calvin. The latter is better known, but he mostly fine-tuned and organized Luther's and Zwingli's ideas. The central points appear over and over among all the Reformers: (1) salvation by grace alone received by faith alone, (2) the final authority of Scripture over church tradition, and (3) the priesthood of every believer.

Like other Reformers, Zwingli spread his ideas through books and pamphlets. His *Commentary on True and False Religion*, the first Reformed systematic theology, was a Protestant manifesto that greatly influenced the direction of the Reformation. He left his mark mostly through Calvin and the Puritans of England and New England, laying much of the foundation for what would become America. God used Zwingli in ways he never expected, just as God does us.

The Radical Reformation

Today we can hardly believe that anybody should be killed for their religious beliefs. In fact, killing someone over religion may be the ultimate barbaric act. But from their beginning the Anabaptists faced persecution and death. You have probably heard of Baptists, but who are Anabaptists? The name simply refers to a rebaptizer, someone who baptizes a second time—a dangerous notion in the sixteenth century, when infant baptism was practiced by Catholics and Reformers alike.

The Reformers are classified in two broad groups: the well-known Magisterial Reformers, including Luther, Zwingli, and Calvin; and the Radical Reformers, who didn't think the first group went far enough. The latter were a collection of Anabaptist groups who spun off of Zwingli's movement and pushed the Reformation to the limit, and maybe beyond.

Zwingli's followers and the Zürich city council tried to implement some Reformation ideals. But their progress was too slow for some, who didn't like the government messing with church affairs anyway. Zwingli was willing to be patient, but when some of his more zealous disciples had enough, they started a home Bible study and refused to baptize their babies. The city council ordered them to stop, but they believed that baptism was only for people who consciously believed in Christ, so they rejected infant baptism. On January 21, 1525, they met to baptize one another as adults, severing all ties with Zwingli and the government.

They believed each Christian could interpret the Bible personally, so they usually avoided formal training and even deep thinking, resulting at times in doctrinal chaos and wild excess. Despite a lack of theological structure, several distinctive beliefs can be noted: baptism by immersion of believing adults rather than sprinkling of children; complete separation of church and state, which led to pacifism; an emphasis on personal salvation and a life of discipleship; and church government in which everyone had an equal voice. These views were dynamite in the political and social structure of the sixteenth century, so Anabaptists were forced underground.

One group set up a communal camp at Münster from 1534 to 1535, expecting Christ's millennium at any time. Some of them claimed to receive divine prophecies and began to apply Old Testament principles without considering the context of the passages. They even crowned a "King David" and introduced polygamy. Strange indeed!

Both Protestant and Catholic officials responded harshly to these fanatics by killing them. Abandoning their normal pacifism, the revolutionaries fought back, but they were hunted down and killed, and their children were given to other families. Survivors fled across Europe, and the movement spread, mostly among the lower classes. The legacy of those early Anabaptists continues today among Mennonites, Hutterites, Amish, Quakers, Brethren, and Baptists.

Anabaptists were hated then, but some of their beliefs are taken for granted today. For example, their notion of separation of church and state is applauded by nearly all. Today, however, it is often twisted into prohibiting religion outside the home and church—an interpretation the Anabaptists never meant.

We also learn from them to endure and serve one another when rejected and persecuted even by other Christians. If their treatment was a black eye on the face of church history, fighting among Christians today still is. The world looks at our infighting and wonders why anyone wants Christianity. The irony is that Jesus taught the opposite: love one another.

The Father of the English Bible

Because God didn't reveal His Word in English, we who speak that language can thank Him for those who translated it for us, starting with John Wycliffe. But the Wycliffe Bible was translated from the Latin Vulgate, which was itself a translation from the original Hebrew and Greek. The need remained for an English version translated directly from the original languages.

William Tyndale possessed translator's gifts: a fine intellect and personal discipline. He received his bachelor's degree at eighteen from Oxford and his master's degree three years later. Then, and later at Cambridge, he demonstrated his linguistic aptitude by mastering French, German, and Italian, and learning Greek, Hebrew, and Latin.

He knew that the allegorical method of interpreting the Bible allowed the Roman Church to protect itself from the common people. If the Bible's truth was hidden in allegories, the people couldn't find it, especially in languages they didn't know. As a result, Rome ruled unchallenged, so Tyndale's passion for an English Bible was an attack on Rome.

When he was ordained, Tyndale was stunned to discover the ignorance of many priests. The fiery English scholar told one who reacted to this opinion, "If God spares my life, before many years pass, I will make it possible for a boy behind the plow to know more Scripture than you do." When the English king prohibited translating the Bible into English, Tyndale chose to break the law, going into exile on the European continent.

In 1525 in Worms, Germany, he published his English New Testament, translated directly from Erasmus's Greek New Testament. Within months, sympathetic merchants were smuggling it into England in barrels of flour and bolts of cloth. Opponents bought and burned all the copies they could find. Tyndale used the profits to print more copies, and he began translating the Old Testament.

For nine years he evaded authorities and continued his work in Europe. English agents pursued him because the Crown didn't want a repeat of the trouble caused by Wycliffe and his followers. Eventually, in 1536 near Antwerp, Tyndale was betrayed, accused of heresy, and thrown into prison.

After seventeen months of cold, lonely misery, he was taken to the public square, tied to a stake with a rope around his neck, and given a chance to recant. Instead, he prayed, "Lord, open the king of England's eyes." The rope was tightened, the fire was lit, and Tyndale died a martyr's death at the age of forty-two. But God answered his prayer, and within a year King Henry VIII approved an English Bible that he didn't know was 70 percent derived from Tyndale's work.

Tyndale's efforts led to other, even better translations and eventually to the King James Version (KJV), the standard for three and a half centuries. Ninety percent of the words of the KJV were taken directly from Tyndale, and his translation was the basis for nearly all English translations until the twentieth century.

God's enemies know how powerful His Word is, and they will kill to keep it from the people. William Tyndale died so we could read God's Book. Opponents killed God's man, but His Word lives on. Let's not waste Tyndale's sacrifice by apathy or neglect.

THOMAS CRANMER (1489–1556)

The English Reformation

No big name like Luther or Calvin is tied to the English Reformation. The best-known figure, Thomas Cranmer, is barely known, and at times he vacillated under pressure. But in the end, this quiet, bookish man guided the English Reformation and changed the course of history.

His father's small landholdings could provide for only one son, so Thomas (the second son) and his younger brother were destined for the priesthood. At fourteen he was sent to Cambridge, where he graduated thirty-second out of forty-two. Despite this modest academic record, he was appointed fellow at Jesus College, Cambridge, in 1510. But when he married the daughter of a tavern owner, his fellowship was revoked. After his wife died in childbirth, he was restored by the college, pursued a life of study, and was ordained a Catholic priest.

When King Henry VIII sought Church approval to divorce Catherine so he could marry a woman who would give him a male heir, he was told that Cranmer agreed. Politics being what they were, Cranmer was soon appointed archbishop of Canterbury, a position he held throughout the reigns of Henry VIII, Edward VI, and Queen Mary.

The English Reformation arose in part from Henry's desire for a male heir. When Rome refused his request for a divorce, Henry simply decreed that the church in England was under his own oversight, not the pope's. No Luther-like figure was needed to wrestle with theology, just a politician who took control. Advisers who refused to go along with this ecclesiastical coup d'état were executed. King Henry now had his new wife (Anne Boleyn), his own church (the Church of England), and his own archbishop of Canterbury (Cranmer).

The people and Parliament applauded this theft. Luther's writings had circulated in England and strengthened Wycliffe's residual influence among the masses. Parliament didn't like Rome's taxation and landholdings, so they also backed Henry. Once the king, the Parliament, and the people told Rome to get lost, Cranmer went to work reforming the church.

The political intrigue peaked near the end of Cranmer's life. Edward VI died in 1553, and "Bloody Mary" began her gruesome reign. This queen was devoutly Catholic and tried to reverse the English

Reformation by killing its leaders. Cranmer was imprisoned for months in solitary confinement in the Tower of London and was forced to recant his Reformation views. He wavered during his final weeks, but on his execution day he renounced Roman doctrine and declared the pope as Christ's enemy and the Antichrist. He was immediately burned at the stake.

Cranmer completed Tyndale's dream of an English Bible by convincing Henry to approve and distribute the Great Bible translation. Cranmer wrote its preface, urging everyone to read, memorize, and live by Scripture. But his *Book of Common Prayer* carried his legacy into the future. Its memorable summaries of doctrine have anchored the souls of millions for four hundred years.

Cranmer was a shrewd diplomat, appeasing rulers to achieve his plans. He showed weakness at times but courage when it was needed most. He bent with the political winds so he could change his world. From Thomas Cranmer we learn to work within the ground rules set by the other team when we have no other choice. Better to achieve something in hard circumstances than nothing at all because we can't play the game our way.

IGNATIUS AND THE COUNTER-REFORMATION
(1491–1556)

Rome Strikes Back

Rome didn't take this Reformation business lightly. It fought back, resisting the Reformers and their allegations of corruption and heresy in the Roman Church. Protestant successes forced Rome to look at abuses within but also spawned the Counter-Reformation. More people and events were included in the Counter-Reformation than Ignatius Loyola, but he's a great place to start.

Ignatius was born in a castle in the Pyrenees, owned by his wealthy Basque family. After living a playboy's life, he became a soldier and was badly injured in 1521 while fighting the French. During his long recovery, he reflected on his past and read two books—one on the life of Christ, the other on lives of the saints. His conclusion differed dramatically from that of Luther, who believed that human will was bound to sin. Ignatius thought people could choose between God and Satan and that increased discipline could help the choice. As a result of this time of reflection, he left his military career and gave his life to the Church as Christ's soldier.

Ignatius spent the next year at Manresa monastery, consecrating himself to Christ, and the next decade in pilgrimage and study at various universities, preparing for service. While in Manresa, he drafted his *Spiritual Exercises*, a course of meditation on the sinfulness of man and the life, death, and resurrection of Christ. Based on his own spiritual journey, it was intended to aid others in their devotion. In time it became mandatory reading for those desiring to enter the Society of Jesus, or the Jesuits.

In 1539 Ignatius asked permission from Pope Paul III to establish a new religious order. The okay came a year later, and the Jesuits began as a military-style order of the church. Ignatius saw them as soldiers of Christ, willing to obey the pope's every command. Their purpose was to return the Church of Rome to its previous spiritual and political power. Handpicked monks received special training for the purposes of teaching children, giving spiritual direction, and sending missionaries abroad. These relentless warriors of the Church often defended the interests of native peoples in foreign lands, but they sometimes justified any means to achieve their end. Defenders praised them, while critics cursed them as the shock troops of the Counter-Reformation.

In addition to blessing the formation of the Society of Jesus, Rome resurrected the Inquisition to counter the Reformation. It had started three centuries before, mostly in Spain, to protect the Church from heretics. In 1542 Cardinal Caraffa urged the pope to use it again, which he did. Caraffa was appointed one of six Inquisitor Generals and later became pope. The accused were presumed guilty and were often tortured to gain a confession. Whether guilty or not, unless they confessed and recanted, they were imprisoned or killed. The result was that The Inquisition did slow the spread of Protestantism.

Ignatius was the most powerful person in Rome's Counter-Reformation, and in 1622 Pope Pius XI canonized him as a saint. To this day, Ignatius is both praised and deplored, but Catholics and Protestants alike benefit privately and in guided retreats from his *Spiritual Exercises*.

JOHN CALVIN (1509–1564)

The Reformation Organizer

Great people are often loved and despised—and for the same reasons. Like Luther, John Calvin was one of the most loved and hated men in history. Luther, the monk-professor, was the fiery revolutionary of the first Reformation generation; Calvin, the lawyer-scholar, was the cool systematizer of the next generation. They never met, but Calvin revered the German Reformer and organized the Protestant thinking that Luther sparked.

Calvin was born in Noyon, sixty miles northeast of Paris. He planned to be a lawyer like his father and at fourteen he enrolled at the University of Paris. Unlike many college students, he actually studied, reading voraciously and thinking deeply. En route to earning his master's degree in 1528, he displayed the genius for logical argument and brilliant writing that later made him famous. In Paris he encountered Reformation ideas, rejected the "superstitions" of Rome, and redirected his studies away from law and classics and toward the Bible and Protestant theology.

Persecution against Protestants forced him to flee

to Basel, Switzerland, where he sought a tranquil life to study and write. While there, at age twenty-seven, he wrote the first edition of his *Institutes of the Christian Religion.* His simple, logical explanation of Reformed beliefs brought him fame across Europe. The next year, while traveling to Strasbourg, he stopped for the night in Geneva. But William Farel, Geneva's leading Protestant, convinced him to stay and build a Reformation church. Calvin reluctantly agreed.

The Geneva city council gave him the title "Professor of Sacred Scripture," and he began to organize the city around Reformed principles. But his rigorous discipline proved more than the political leaders bargained for, so he and Farel were forced to leave. Three years later his friends convinced him to return, and before long, Reformation-minded Christians from across Europe fled to Geneva, "the Protestant Rome."

For the rest of his life, Calvin preached verse by verse through books of the Bible, applying its truths to his hearers' lives. For all his deep theological thinking, he was highly practical. As he approached death, he told his followers to bury his body in a common grave marked by a simple stone so no one could turn it into a shrine. He died on May 27, 1564, and they did as he asked. Today no one knows where his grave is.

Calvin arranged the Reformers' beliefs, especially Zwingli's, around the theme of God's sovereignty. He revised and expanded his *Institutes* throughout his life, and they remain the classic expression of Reformation theology. Because his system incorporated a whole worldview, he influenced politics, law, economics, art, and nearly every other part of society across Europe and early America. One way or another, his work shaped Reformed, Presbyterian, Congregational, Anglican, and some Baptist traditions. American Puritans set up their "godly commonwealth" based in part on Calvin's Geneva.

If Augustine's was the greatest Christian mind of the first millennium, John Calvin's has been called the greatest of the second. A lifetime of service may lead to love or loathing, but it makes an impact. Whether or not one agrees with Calvin's theology, may we emulate his disciplined, organized way of thinking and apply it with grace and mercy.

Rome Defines Its Doctrine

Enough was enough! Rome had no choice but to reckon with the growing Protestant threat, so in 1537 Pope Paul III called a council to examine the state of the Church. But political delays prevented his plan until he issued a papal bull in 1544 to convene a council at Trent in northern Italy.

The council assembled three times: 1545–1547, 1551–1552, and 1562–1563. Attendees varied from one session to the next, but Italians (loyal to the pope) made up three-quarters of the delegates, so they controlled procedures and carried the votes. Emperor Charles V took the odd step of pressing the Church to include Protestant leaders from Germany. To placate him, a few were invited to the second session, but because they weren't allowed to speak or vote, their presence was meaningless.

The pope asked the council to consider three broad areas: doctrinal issues, clerical abuses, and another crusade. But the different blocks of delegates who gathered at Trent brought their own agendas. Spanish and

48 | THE REFORMATION BEGINS (1517–1563)

French bishops desired more independence from Rome. Jesuits, on the other hand, were protective of the pope's authority. Representatives from within the papal circle resisted any reforms that might have restrained their self-indulgent lifestyles. Emperor Charles V, ever the politician, sought a compromise between Catholics and Protestants (wishful thinking at best).

Predictably, the council rejected everything the Reformers stood for and affirmed the doctrines of medieval Romanism. Trent undercut the central tenet of Protestantism—salvation by grace alone through faith alone—by adding works to earn grace. Furthermore, it compromised the supreme authority of Scripture by asserting that Church tradition was the only way to rightly interpret the Bible. It also affirmed all seven of the Roman sacraments, declaring them necessary for salvation.

After Trent, partaking of the Mass (Communion) was still considered a fresh sacrifice of Christ that satisfied the Father all over again. The council pronounced the Latin Vulgate, including the Apocryphal books, to be the official version of Scripture. It denied the priesthood of all believers and affirmed the hierarchy of Rome. Finally, council members issued a list of prohibited books, rejecting Protestant works and approving strictly

Catholic sources. To its credit, Trent did address and improve some internal Church practices: Clergy should be educated, and they could no longer abuse their privileges.

In 1564 the pope issued a bull summarizing the council's decisions, and all clergy and teachers were forced to accept it. To reject the teachings of Trent was to be a heretic and could result in excommunication. Any remaining hope for unity between Catholics and Protestants was already long gone, but this bull signed the death certificate. With typical zeal for the pope, the Jesuits used the results of Trent to slow Protestant progress anywhere they could.

After Trent, the religious face of Europe was fixed in place; Rome couldn't eradicate Protestants, and Protestants couldn't reform Rome. The result: Europe was divided into two permanent religious populations. Trent was the most important council between Nicaea in 325 and Vatican II in 1962–1965. It forged Rome's response to the Reformation and defined Catholicism for four centuries.

Even Vatican II did not change the decisions of Trent as much as add a new, more mellow attitude. Today, significant differences remain between Catholics and Protestants, but since Vatican II, meaningful dialogue occurs. And at least Catholics and Protestants are talking instead of killing each other.

JOHN KNOX (C. 1513–1572)

The Thundering Scot

When Mary Queen of Scots married into the French royal line, people feared she might give Scotland to France. Opposing such power and corruption called for a fearless man. That man was John Knox, a prickly, cantankerous guy who could alienate anyone—just what God needed to reform Scotland when the Catholic Church owned half the land and earned eighteen times the income of the Crown.

Knox was born into humble surroundings in Haddington, just south of Edinburgh. He majored in theology and law at St. Andrews and Glasgow but never graduated. His upbringing among common people served him well, enabling him to communicate with ordinary folks. He accepted ordination as a Catholic priest in 1536, but when he heard Thomas Guilliame preach Reformed doctrines, he converted to Protestantism.

His new faith so captured his heart that he became a bodyguard for George Wishart, another traveling preacher. Catholic Cardinal Beaton later had Wishart killed—a fate the cardinal himself soon suffered at the hands of Wishart supporters. Knox wasn't involved in the second killing, but he approved of it, and for this he was locked up in St. Andrews Castle along with Beaton's killers.

In a strange twist, the French Navy kidnapped Knox and his roommates from the castle. For nineteen months he was forced to row as a galley slave on a warship. At one point, when ordered to kiss a statue of the Virgin Mary, he avoided committing this "idolatry" by throwing the statue overboard when no one was looking. He was later released in a prisoner exchange but fled to Europe and John Calvin when Mary Tudor ("Bloody Mary") ascended the throne of England.

In 1559 Knox returned to Scotland and promoted a Calvinist-flavored Reformation, attacking everything Catholic. His sermons often consisted of thirty minutes of calm biblical exposition followed by wild, pulpit-pounding application, calling Scots to revolt against Rome. He preached with such passion that on one occasion a riot erupted. Elected pastor of his church in Edinburgh, he continued to fan Protestant flames. Parliament asked him and five cohorts (all named John) to write a confession of faith, which the governing body soon approved, and Catholicism was voted out of Scotland.

When Knox died, he left behind the most Calvinist country on earth. His impact still echoes in the words of Mary Queen of Scots: "I fear the prayers of John Knox more than all the armies of Europe." Knox influenced the New World as well when Scottish Presbyterians migrated to America in the early eighteenth century, infecting Americans with a desire for independence. Today millions of Presbyterians worldwide can trace their spiritual legacy to the thundering Scot.

Knox feared no one—not the queen, the pope, or the people. His rough style reminds us of an Old Testament prophet, not warm and fuzzy but effective in communicating God's truth. He cared nothing for wealth, status, or safety but only for God's mission. He demonstrated a truth we need to hear in today's age of personality cults: neither charisma nor charm is the key to usefulness in the hands of God.

THE HUGUENOTS (SIXTEENTH CENTURY)

French Calvinists

Why does God allow tragedy to strike innocent people? We don't have a final answer to that question, but there's no doubt our fallen world pours out misery on God's people. The French Huguenots must have asked the same question. Their story is one of the saddest in church history.

The origin of the name Huguenot is debated, but French Protestants were called that from about 1560. French-speaking Swiss Calvinists had introduced Reformation ideas into France by 1546, and the first Huguenot church in Paris was formed nine years later. Despite persecution, the movement spread, and nearly two million French, including the famed Admiral Coligny, became Protestant. Tensions with Catholics grew as the numbers of Huguenots increased. France suffered three religious wars in the 1560s. Protestants attacked Catholic property, and Catholics retaliated by killing Protestants. It was an ugly time filled with suspicion and hatred.

Hostilities peaked in 1572 with the St. Bartholomew's Day Massacre. It began with a Paris wedding between Margaret, sister of King Charles IX, and Henry of Navarre, an important Protestant leader. The bride's mother, Catherine de Médicis, and other powerful Catholics were jealous of Admiral Coligny's influence, especially with the king, so they hatched a plan to assassinate the Huguenot leader Coligny. Four days after the wedding, a would-be assassin shot Coligny twice. He survived, only to be stabbed to death while recovering. Huguenot anger engulfed the city. When the conspirators convinced Charles that Protestants would retaliate, he ordered a preemptive strike.

The initial massacre of August 23 and 24 took about two thousand Huguenot lives. The mayhem raced out of control. Over the next six weeks, Paris and a dozen other French cities saw thirty thousand men, women, and children killed and their property seized by order of the Catholic Church. The slaughter was so gruesome that some Catholics hid Protestants in their homes. Meanwhile, Catholics in Rome and Spain celebrated the news of Protestant slaughter, and the pope commissioned a special coin to be minted in honor of the event. The Protestant movement in France never fully recovered.

The repeated religious wars eventually exhausted everyone, and a compromise was sought. The opportunity arose when Henry of Navarre assumed the throne in 1589, causing Catholics in France and Spain to threaten more bloodshed if he didn't convert to Catholicism. He conceded in 1593. But in 1598 he granted legal recognition to Protestants and freedom to practice their religion in parts of France in a treaty called the Edict of Nantes.

A semblance of peace was maintained until Louis XIV revoked the edict a century later and persecution of Protestants resumed. Many Huguenots fled the country, emigrating to other parts of Europe, South Africa, and America. Many had been skilled artisans and professionals in the French middle class, and their absence hurt the French economy.

The French religious wars and the St. Bartholomew's Day Massacre revealed the bigotry and brutality of that era. They changed the religious and political landscape of France so much that even now evangelical missionaries report little response in France. Yet even though the sword may slow the spread of an idea, it seldom kills the idea itself. Displaced Huguenots took their Calvinist doctrine with them, spreading Protestant beliefs to other parts of the world. God allowed them to suffer, but their persecution sent them to places where they probably would not otherwise have gone.

Yet Another Church?

The yellow pages of most American towns list a large number of Baptist churches compared to other types of Protestant churches. And these Baptist churches might belong to a dozen or more varieties of denominations and associations. Why is that? Where did the Baptists come from and how did they get to be the way they are?

The Baptist church began during the religious turmoil of seventeenth-century England. Some Puritans tried to reform the Church of England but became so frustrated that they left. They were thus called Separatists. Eventually, several denominations emerged from among them, including two strains of Baptists.

Some Separatists fled persecution to Holland, where they found a degree of religious freedom. The leader of one group, Cambridge graduate John Smyth, studied the Greek New Testament and did not find infant baptism included in it. So in 1609 he baptized himself and a friend named Thomas Helwys and then all the adult members of his church. When Smyth learned that a local Mennonite church agreed with his view of baptism, he tried to merge his group with theirs. But Helwys disapproved, and in 1612 he and ten others returned to London to form the first Baptist church in England.

The group in Holland had accepted Arminian doctrines and became known as General Baptists. (Arminianism is a system of theology named after theologian Jacob Arminius, which emphasizes human free will.) But in 1633 a more Calvinistic group, later called Particular Baptists, began a church in London under the leadership of John Spilsbury. They were less schismatic and more open to other believers, even allowing Christians from non-Baptist churches to join without being immersed.

English politics contributed to the Baptists' early growth. From 1640 to 1660, Parliament opposed two institutions: an absolute monarchy and a state church. Because Baptists believed the church should be independent of the government, they spread rapidly during this time. By 1660, three hundred Baptist churches existed in England.

In addition to believing that government shouldn't interfere with churches, Baptists held several other signature convictions. They believed that Scripture is the final authority, that church membership is only for confessing Christians, that only "adult" believers (that is, those old enough to profess their faith in Christ) should be baptized, and that all believers should share in church ministry and decisions.

The most obvious symbol of Baptist faith was and is adult baptism by immersion rather than the sprinkling of infants. In the seventeenth century (and still today in some places), this was a radical act of defiance. It deviated from more than a thousand years of tradition in most of the Christian world. For centuries, infant baptism was the means of enlisting everyone on the church rolls and into the greater society. So some Christians thought the foundation of the church and the civilized world was threatened when Baptists immersed adults instead of sprinkling their babies.

At times Baptist independence has led to church tension. And in Baptist circles, because every person has equal voice (at least in principle), every opinion carries equal weight. The Baptist reputation for internal fights and church splits has been well earned; Baptist churches often multiply by dividing. But that same independent spirit has promoted evangelism and global missions. Thousands of Baptist churches are found worldwide as a result of outreach. We can learn from their zeal even as we avoid a schismatic spirit.

THE KING JAMES BIBLE (1611)

Good Enough for Paul?

You may have heard someone say, "If the King James Version was good enough for Paul, it's good enough for me." Unfortunately, that view is more than a joke; a few people actually believe the great apostle used the King James Version. Who was King James, and why does one Bible bear his name?

James, the son of Mary Queen of Scots, was King James VI of Scotland. But in 1603 he succeeded Queen Elizabeth of England as James I, uniting the two kingdoms for the first time. He ascended the throne when Puritans were trying to "purify" the church from all remnants of Catholicism. When Puritan leaders met with him at Hampton Court in 1604 to ask his help in reforming the church, he declined. But he agreed to one request: a new translation of the Bible. They all agreed that the current versions were not accurate to the original Hebrew and Greek.

The most popular Bible was the Geneva Bible, but James didn't like it because he thought it sounded too Calvinistic. Another popular Bible was the Bishop's

Bible, but most of the common people didn't care for it. England needed a new, more accurate translation that would satisfy as many people as possible.

King James didn't write, translate, or do any work on the King James Version. He merely appointed fifty scholars and divided them into groups to do the work. The text was doled out in six sections corresponding to the six teams of translators. They were directed to modify previous English versions and make changes only when the Greek or Hebrew demanded it. Therefore the KJV is a reworking of existing versions more than a new translation.

The final product was an improvement but not what we today would expect from a fresh translation working straight from the original languages. Furthermore, the available Greek and Hebrew manuscripts were limited and the translators' expertise was marginal. The common identification of the KJV as the "Authorized Version" does not mean it is superior to other translations. That title, in fact, is not strictly accurate, because no evidence has been found that King James formally authorized the final product.

Nearly a half-century passed before the KJV overcame the Geneva Bible in popularity, but in time it was accepted by the masses. It remained the most-used version among English-speaking Protestants until the Revised Version came out in the 1880s. By the 1960s, the increased availability of Greek and Hebrew manuscripts revealed the KJV's errors, opening the door for numerous better translations. Also, by then its archaic language rendered it nearly obsolete except among people who grew up with it or just preferred the style of the language.

The language of the KJV is not and never was more godly than any other. It was simply the English of the early seventeenth century. The mystique some people find in its phrasing is a matter of preference and familiarity. God has used the KJV to change millions of lives over three and a half centuries, and today He uses more accurate and more readable translations to change millions more. We can thank Him for both.

ENGLISH PURITANS (SIXTEENTH AND
SEVENTEENTH CENTURIES)

The Pre-Americans

Mention Puritans to most Americans and they reply
with disgust, "Weren't they that dreary bunch of self-
righteous moralists who hated sex and fun and started
everything that's messed up about America today?"
Actually, no. That worn-out image is wrong on all
counts. The Puritans wore colorful clothes with ribbons
and lace; enjoyed good music and books; drank rum
and beer; skated, swam, and bowled; and (judging from
the size of their families) knew what to do on cold winter
nights.

But from the start they got a bad rap, smeared as
"Puritans" by their religious opponents in the 1560s for
trying to reform or "purify" the Church of England, which
they believed was still too Catholic. They were simply
English Protestants who tried, unsuccessfully, to transform the Anglican Church and the English state into
something like Calvin's Geneva. Persecution peaked after
Queen Elizabeth I enacted a law requiring attendance at
Anglican churches. Despite the threat of imprisonment,

many Puritans refused to attend churches they considered tainted by Catholicism. King James I then swore that he would make them conform or run them out—or worse! Repression finally drove many from England to Holland, which allowed nonconformity.

The Puritans' theology was their own unique flavor of Calvinism, starting with the glory of a sovereign God. Learning and living His Word was the all-in-all of Puritan life. The pinnacle of the week was the sermon; Puritans demanded deep and practical Bible-based preaching from their pastors, and they got it. Their passion to reform the church arose from the Bible, which they studied and obeyed as if their lives depended on it—a shocking notion to some of their neighbors, who loved religious tradition more than God's truth.

Puritans were not illiterate country bumpkins; indeed, they were a highly educated, thinking people. They wielded influence in and through Cambridge University and produced many leading early scientists. Seven of the ten men behind the Royal Society of London were Puritans, even though Puritans made up only a fraction of the total population.

No Puritan church exists in England today. Puritanism thrived for about a century, then fragmented, its remnant represented by a few who remained in the

Anglican Church and many others who drifted into non-conformist groups: Congregationalists, Presbyterians, and Baptists. Their greatest legacy was born in 1620 as about a hundred of them boarded a small ship to cross the western ocean to a new and unknown world. No one back home could have guessed what would grow from that tiny band of feisty Calvinists. The prevailing attitude was "Good riddance!"

Other Europeans of the time were going to find new lands because they dreamed of wealth from trading goods. Puritan incentives for emigration included the freedom to worship as they wished, opportunities to evangelize everyone they met, and the desire to build a new world to the glory of God. For now we leave them on the high seas of the North Atlantic, fighting the autumn winds and praying for survival. We will meet them again.

We can barely begin to list the lessons the Puritans left behind. If we set aside our bias and explore who and what they were, we discover the following among their many traits: humility before a holy God, courage to stand alone for truth, effort exerted to enhance His glory, and deep thinking in the service of others. Those traits may have fallen on hard times in today's world, but we would do well to seek them all to the glory of God.

THE WESTMINSTER CONFESSION (1646)

A Glorious Summary

Christians believe the Bible is God's Word, sufficient to know Him and know how to live for His glory. They mine its pages to discover specific beliefs of their faith. But the Bible is a long and sometimes complex book, so most churches summarize their core beliefs in a doctrinal statement, or statement of faith. One of the best known is the Westminster Confession of Faith, the classic summary of Reformed theology in English. We might assume that it came from Calvin or his followers in Geneva, but actually it was drafted a century later by English and Scottish Christians.

During the mid-1600s, English Puritans controlled Parliament, removed King Charles I, and set up a republic under Oliver Cromwell. In the midst of those turbulent times, Parliament convened a council to advise them on religious issues. That council, the Westminster Assembly, was given the task of revising the Thirty-Nine Articles, the religious convictions approved by Parliament in the previous century to address the religious issues of that day.

In 1643 a total of 151 English Puritans and Scottish Presbyterians gathered at London's Westminster Abbey. Many wanted to redesign the English church into a Reformed national Church of England like the Scottish Presbyterian Church. Parliament had promised the Scots that they would do that in exchange for military support against King Charles. That particular goal wasn't achieved, however, because not all attendees agreed, and Episcopal leaders refused to attend at all.

The assembly met almost daily, more than a thousand times between 1643 and 1648. They weren't authorized to make decisions, only recommendations to give to Parliament. In December 1646 they completed their main task, the Westminster Confession of Faith. To aid churches in training their people in doctrine, they also designed two teaching aids, called the longer and shorter catechisms. English and Scottish parliaments soon approved the assembly's work, and these three documents became standard guides for Presbyterians, Puritans, and others.

The Westminster Confession of Faith was so well received that it was soon used as the basis for other doctrinal confessions, especially among Congregationalists and some Baptists. In the early twentieth century, during the modernist/fundamentalist debate, conservative scholar J. Gresham Machen relied on it to expose liberal theology as a completely different religion rather than just another variation of Christianity. With only minor modifications, the confession and the catechisms taken from it have endured to this day as the doctrinal summary of many churches.

The Westminster Confession is one of the time-honored hallmarks of evangelical Christianity. Because it was produced only one generation after the King James Bible, its language is not always easy to understand. A version with updated language, but without changes in doctrine, has been produced to help modern readers and students.

Many Christians have heard the first point of the Shorter Catechism: "Question: 'What is the chief end of man?' Answer: 'To glorify God and enjoy Him forever.'" Few Christians of any stripe would dislike that opening to this wonderful doctrinal summary. The Shorter Catechism still provides a great starting point for churches to use in training converts and for parents to use with their children.

THE THIRTY YEARS WAR (1618–1648)

A Marathon of Fighting

No fight matches a church fight, and no war rivals a religious war. The ugliest atrocities are committed and condoned by people who believe they are fighting for God. The events of September 11, 2001 graphically illustrate the point.

Similarly, the Reformation began as a dialogue over theology but eventually led to armed conflict. Post-Reformation Europe experienced three decades of brutality when full-scale war broke out among differing Christian groups. The Thirty Years War was a series of four related conflicts between Protestant and Catholic forces in Central Europe.

A complex set of religious, political, and economic factors, stirred by mutual hatred and fear, set the stage. Tensions ran high, awaiting a spark to explode. In 1618 Catholic Ferdinand II became king of Bohemia, the land of pre-Protestant martyr Jan Hus. When Ferdinand tried to replace Protestantism with Catholicism, Bohemian nobles rebelled and pledged their loyalty to German ruler Frederick V, a committed Calvinist. He accepted, and the war was on.

The war was fought in four phases. The Bohemian stage (1618–1623) was Ferdinand's conquest of the Bohemians and Frederick's forces. The Danish stage (1625–1629) began when Christian IV of Denmark tried to protect northern Germany from the Bohemians' fate and gain land for himself. He failed and was driven back home. The Swedish stage (1630–1635) started with King Gustavus Adolphus's invasion of Germany. His well-trained army won victory after victory, but when Gustavus was killed in battle, his troops withdrew. The final stage (1635–1648) commenced when Catholic France attacked a weakened Germany to expand its territory.

By this point the seemingly endless war was more political than religious. Neither side could defeat the other, and the conflict finally wore down from exhaustion. Germany was devastated, nearly one-third of its population dead. Much of the continent was ravaged and the people's taste for blood was more than satisfied. Such carnage would not return to Europe for three hundred years, when World War I erupted.

In a series of discussions from 1643 to 1648 the weary combatants drafted an agreement called the Treaty of Westphalia, named after the province where they met. The notion of a universal religious state gave way to sovereign nations where people could believe what they wanted. National rulers would allow Protestants and Catholics to mix at will, and the pope couldn't call the political shots.

A new world was dawning, and the pope was no longer the linchpin in its politics. When Pope Innocent X objected, no one listened. Nations that avoided the conflict, including England, benefited by growing their fleets and establishing colonies as bases for foreign trade. They became the power players of the next age as their depleted, war-ravaged neighbors lay prone on the bloody soil of Europe.

Whatever differences arise among religions, killing one another doesn't address the issues or resolve the problems. The hardest challenge comes when one side believes that killing others is legitimate and virtuous. Fortunately, most people today recognize the hard-fought lesson of the Thirty Years War: we can live side by side in peace.

A City on a Hill

Two months at sea left our Puritan passengers on the *Mayflower* desperate for land. They left England aiming for Virginia but landed far north at Plymouth Rock. Frustrated with the Church of England, thousands more came to the New World in the coming decades. One shipload in 1630 heard a prophetic sermon from John Winthrop about the world watching them like a city on a hill.

The Puritans fled England to find religious freedom, but they didn't start New England to allow people to believe whatever they chose. The first two generations of Americans expected religious conformity, as had the rulers back home. But the Puritans allowed dissenters to leave without persecution; the New World was a big place with room for all who wanted to believe and live a different way.

The driving passion of the American Puritans was spiritual birth and growth. Their first steps of building a new world included learning, writing, and publishing theology, and founding a college to train pastors. They also loved their neighbors, the Indians. Without Indian help, the Puritans might not have survived beyond the first brutal winter, which wiped out nearly half the group.

Puritans honored the mind. When Massachusetts was still new, it could boast more than a hundred Oxford and Cambridge grads, leading one historian to call it the best-educated society in history. Education began at home with mothers teaching children to read and write. Secondary schools taught classics to prepare young men for college. Ministers were trained at Cambridge. Puritans believed God's grace entered the heart through the mind, and the minister who didn't study and teach the Bible was derelict in his duty.

Their two-hour sermons were biblically based, theologically sophisticated, and logically organized—not for the spiritually faint of heart. Most sermons followed the same format: explanation of a biblical text, followed by expansion of a central doctrine in that passage, and then application to life. Puritan pastors were well trained and fiercely protective of their study time. Most of their waking hours were spent in their libraries while they prepared and wrote their sermons verbatim. The Puritans referred to the untrained and ill prepared as "dumme dogs," unfit to preach.

To avoid "dumme dogs" and rely less on England for ministers, just seven years after arriving they founded a college to train their own ministers. They named it after the man who gave his library and half his estate to start it: John Harvard. Future pastors studied Scripture, classical languages, philosophy, and physics. William and Mary, Yale, Princeton, Columbia, Brown, and Dartmouth soon followed.

To a large extent, the Puritan legacy *is* America. In 1776, when the colonists told England to buzz off, 75 percent of them were from Puritan stock. Our passion for excellence, education, government, ethics, and virtue began in their vision of God and His command to improve the world for His glory. It's only a slight exaggeration to say that most of the good in America began with the Puritans and most of the bad has come from rejecting their worldview.

The Puritans weren't perfect; they had their quirks. But in their pursuit of spiritual maturity, they sought discipline and virtue rather than ease and pleasure. Their souls possessed depth and inner gravity, and they lived life as though it mattered. More of that is needed today.

JOHN MILTON (1608–1674)

The Second Blind Bard

The Iliad and *The Odyssey* of Homer, the blind bard of ancient Greece, have survived three thousand years, proving their worth as immortal classics. Shortly after Shakespeare's time, a blind English Puritan named John Milton wrote theology in the same form that Homer wrote: epic poetry. It survives to this day. Three hundred years is not three thousand, but it's a good start.

Milton was born to a wealthy London family. His literary abilities soon appeared as he and his tutor compared poetry they wrote in Latin and Greek. Despite eye problems as a child, John was an avid reader. His brother later recalled that John often stayed up late reading and writing poetry worthy of a much older person. While training at Cambridge, he continued his poetry in Latin, Italian, and English. A few of his minor works were published even before he considered writing as a career. After receiving a master's degree, he returned home to live off his family's wealth, studying music and writing more poetry for the next five years.

Thoughts of writing epic poetry came to his mind while he was traveling in Europe. But rumors of civil war in England brought him home to London, where he started a private academy for aristocratic children. He was planning a grand epic based on King Arthur's legend when war broke out between Oliver Cromwell and King Charles I. Milton surrendered his talents to Cromwell by writing political pamphlets for his Puritan cause. He argued for the rights of the people, even the right to remove and punish tyrants. After Charles I was executed, Milton was appointed secretary of foreign languages in Cromwell's government, a position that required him to correspond with officials in other nations, usually in Latin.

His eyesight worsened until he went completely blind in 1652. He was able to keep his job by dictating to a secretary, but Cromwell's government came to an end and Charles II ascended to the throne. Milton went into hiding to avoid arrest, but he was found, imprisoned, and fined for opposing the Crown. He escaped worse punishment because the new king wanted to ingratiate himself with the people by sparing the old, blind poet whose works were now well known.

Milton had dreamed of writing an epic poem in the style of Homer about Satan's revolt in heaven and Adam and Eve's fall in the garden. In 1658 he set about this massive task, which took five years to finish. *Paradise*

Lost was finally published in ten books in 1667, then in a twelve-book second version in 1674. *Paradise Regained* came out four years later.

Milton's enduring work made him one of England's greatest poets, though his reputation never matched that of William Shakespeare, who died when Milton was seven. Nevertheless, he influenced writers to our day, including J. R. R. Tolkien, author of THE LORD OF THE RINGS trilogy. Some have suggested that Milton's blindness enhanced his literary abilities by stimulating his imagination. Maybe that was Homer's key to greatness as well.

Art is an expression of God's image within us. Our creative abilities are far less than His, but He planted them in us to magnify Himself. Milton's epic poetry, patterned after Homer's, graphically recounts one of the Bible's great stories and deserves a reading by every Christian. Every time it's read, we can glorify God, who planted the gift of literary creativity in the second blind bard.

The Puritan Titan

A few Christians believe the misguided notion that great scholars can't love God. John Owen, the titan of English Puritans, proves them wrong. A godly scholar, leader, and writer, he championed Reformed orthodoxy in all his work, always revealing the passion of his heart: communion with the living God.

Owen came from Celtic blood and was the son of the Puritan vicar in Stradham. Having entered Oxford at age twelve, he received his BA at sixteen and his MA at nineteen. During those academic years, he damaged his health by allowing himself only four hours of sleep per night so that he might study and learn as much as he could. Compelled by godly ambition, he drove himself to do something worthy with his life. But he left Oxford in 1637 over a disagreement with the chancellor. Hopes of a bright career, academic or otherwise, were dampened, but God wasn't finished with him.

Owen's achievements exceed what might be expected of two or three people: pastor of several London churches; mediator between Presbyterian and

Congregational Puritans; chaplain for Oliver Cromwell on campaigns in Ireland and Scotland; regular speaker at Parliament, including the day after King Charles was executed; Oxford's Member of Parliament for a short time; dean and vice chancellor at Oxford; prolific writer of theology; and father of eleven children, ten of whom died when young. He declined offers to become pastor of First Church of Boston as well as president of Harvard and several Dutch universities. In recognition of his life's work, Oxford eventually conferred on him an honorary doctor of divinity degree. After years of suffering from asthma and gallstones, he died in 1683.

Owen possessed a remarkable mind, able to grasp and organize vast amounts of information and put it on paper. He wrote throughout his life, publishing eighty works, some of them massive. Most are still in print, mentoring Christians today. His commentary on Hebrews—a multivolume set laboriously written and published over sixteen years—displays the finest tools of seventeenth-century scholarship.

Owen's legacy grew out of his inner passion for God, not his public ministry. Personal communion with God fed him, drove him, sustained him. Like all Puritans, but more than most, Owen's daily sustenance was prayer and meditation. His love of learning was but a tool for knowing and fellowshipping with the God he loved so much. Learning was the means, not the end, for his mind, his heart, and his life. Many Christian leaders today honor Owen as a great influence in their lives. More Christians might do so if they knew the impact he made on their pastors and those who mentor them.

In all his seeking of God, Owen never departed from the Word. He knew that God revealed Himself in Scripture, and this was the source that Owen mined for His presence. How different from us today! If we desire God at all, it's often apart from sweet labor in His Word, thinking God just appears because we desire mystical thrills. Our interest in God seems but a shadow compared to John Owen's relentless pursuit of the Holy One. May we capture the passionate depth of his life and seek the living God he knew so well.

BLAISE PASCAL (1623–1662)

Original Thinker

Now and then a genius appears on the landscape of humanity. Most of these rare people think outside the box in one area of life. Blaise Pascal thought outside all the boxes. He lived during the Age of Reason—the Enlightenment—and no one's ability to reason exceeded his. He earned a reputation as a mathematician, scientist, inventor, philosopher, mystic, and apologist, and he excelled in all these areas.

Pascal was born into a Catholic family, the son of a civil servant in Clermont-Ferrand, France. His mother died when he was three, so his father assumed the task of educating the children. Dad fed his son's curiosity by taking him to meetings of the Academy of Science, and it paid off. Even as a youth, Pascal made original discoveries in mathematics. But until he was fifteen, his father hid the math books to force him to study languages too. Pascal responded by working out thirty-two of Euclid's propositions, which he didn't previously know existed, and Dad gave in.

Pascal was converted from nominal Catholicism

to Jansenism—a Christian branch that believed in Calvinistic doctrines previously taught by Augustine. He learned that life's mystery and suffering met its match in God's wondrous grace. He pored over the Bible, seeking answers to life's most vexing questions, found peace in Christ, and began a life of deep reflection. After his death, a servant found a scribbled note in Pascal's coat lining that recorded a mystical experience from eight years earlier, referred to as "a night of fire." Pascal had never told anyone about it because for him it never replaced the revelation of Scripture.

His career could fill a volume of *Who's Who.* He was one of the world's great scientists in physics and math, especially probability theory, which he developed to help his friends gamble. Mathematicians considered his geometry book too advanced to have been written by a teenager, but it was. He invented the first calculator when he was nineteen to help his father, who was a tax collector at the time. He figured out the principles of atmospheric pressure and the equilibrium of fluids needed for hydraulic systems. He even invented the vacuum cleaner and the wristwatch and designed a transit system for Paris centuries before buses existed.

Pascal died at thirty-nine, having just begun to make notes for a monumental book on Christian apologetics.

Fortunately for us, friends collected those notes and published them eight years later as *Pensées* (*Thoughts*). It bears a rough resemblance to the *Confessions* of Augustine, whom Pascal greatly admired. Filled with profound insight into human existence, it is considered one of the greatest books of all time. He presents human beings as wretched creatures who can be transformed by faith in God's grace through Christ. Evidence for God is plentiful but worthless without faith, which God Himself gives.

Pascal was ahead of his time in apologetics as well as in physics and math. From three centuries ago, the maverick genius still guides us on our spiritual journey. Regarded by some as the greatest French stylist, his thoughts are so profound that even his rough notes became an enduring classic. God still uses people who think originally.

The Greatest Story Ever Retold

Invented stories can never replace God's Word, but Bible-based tales can drive God's truth into the soul, inspiring us to greater faith. The writer of one of the most enduring stories was John Bunyan, another English Puritan preacher. He was born in Elstow, the eldest son of a tinsmith, a little-regarded profession in England. His education matched his station in life: no university training for this poor tinker's son. As a youth, he lived a rough, undisciplined life, his colossal talents lying dormant.

About 1653, influenced by Luther's commentary on Galatians and by Pastor John Gillford of the Baptist Church in Bedford, Bunyan trusted Christ for salvation. Within a few years, he began to preach at a time when preaching by nonconformists (non-Anglicans) was banned by the newly restored monarchy. His gifts flourished; people listened; the authorities panicked; and Bunyan found himself in prison. Before and during his jail time, he was given the offer of freedom in exchange for agreeing not to preach. He refused, thereby extending his sentence from three months to eleven years.

Solitary suffering was the furnace God stoked in Bunyan's soul, resulting in some of the greatest writing of all time. Indeed, during the 1660s, all Puritan scholars, writers, and preachers were banned from universities and pulpits. The pen was the only outlet for their spiritual passion, so they wrote on the run and in their cells, and we are blessed because of it. Even before Bunyan's release in 1672, the Bedford church called him as their pastor. He later refused calls to London so he could remain in Bedford. In 1688, following a rain-drenched horse ride to London, he came down with a fever and died.

Bunyan's legacy lies in his writing (over sixty books), especially *Pilgrim's Progress*, an allegory of the spiritual journey. Using homespun paraphrases of the Bible, he maneuvered the character "Christian" along a harrowing journey from the City of Destruction to the Celestial City across the river. Few can read it without finding themselves in it again and again. Next to the Bible, *Pilgrim's Progress* was the most loved book in England, reprinted a dozen times in the decade after its release in 1678.

When King Charles II asked John Owen (see essay

58) how he could listen to the preaching of an illiterate tinker, Owen said he would gladly give up his learning if he could preach like Bunyan. A century later the great evangelist George Whitefield wrote the preface to the 1767 reprint of *Pilgrim's Progress.* As English believers rounded the globe in the missionary explosion of the nineteenth century, they first translated the Bible, then *Pilgrim's Progress.*

It now comes in over one hundred languages and ranks second only to the Bible on the all-time bestseller list. God still uses it to guide spiritual explorers today, teaching us how to live and fight for joy in a broken world and how to die well. God used the writing of learned scholars like Owen and common tinkers like Bunyan. Writing is one expression of the teaching gift that the church should discover, develop, and honor.

THE PIETISTS
(SEVENTEENTH AND EIGHTEENTH CENTURIES)

Religion of the Heart

Integrating head and heart has always challenged the church. Throughout history the pendulum has swung back and forth between knowing and feeling. Reaction and overreaction have led to extremes of dry intellectualism and wild-eyed mysticism. One reaction (some would say overreaction) to post-Reformation scholasticism was Pietism.

The Pietist movement began in Germany in response to the dead, formal orthodoxy that Lutheranism slipped into a century after the great Reformer. The Pietists agreed with Luther and what he did. They even thought they were the second phase of his Reformation. But they didn't think he went far enough—not in terms of certain doctrines, as Anabaptists thought, but in the realm of the heart. Pietism never was a denomination or particular group but rather a perspective, a way of seeing and living the Christian life that crossed denominations and still exists in most of them today.

By the late seventeenth century, in some Reformation

circles, the God-honoring use of the mind descended into a cold, spiritless orthodoxy of passive assent to finely tuned doctrines. As the Reformation fires cooled, the vibrancy of Luther and Calvin and others was replaced by rigid formulas and church rituals. Pietists tried to recapture the experiential part of the Christian faith, and the pendulum began to swing the other way, back toward the heart.

They wanted to recenter the Christian life in the living God and away from the state church. They stressed personal conversion, individual and small-group Bible study, holy living, evangelism, and missions—most of which were present in Puritanism. But in the process they demoted doctrine and added a subjective, human-centered element that had never invaded the Puritans' God-focused outlook. One's *experience* in the Bible became equal to the *truth* in the Bible (hints of twentieth-century neoorthodoxy? See essay 84).

Pietism wielded a huge influence, revitalizing many denominations. Perhaps its best contribution was jump-starting the modern missions movement, especially through the eighteenth-century Moravians, the first to cross the water with the gospel. (We'll meet them in essay 63.) It also tilled the spiritual soil of England and America, preparing them for future awakenings.

But Pietism also introduced weaknesses, as all movements do. Elevating experience above the mind led to sentimentalism and, in severe cases, to unbiblical mysticism. Modern liberal theology, born in the nineteenth century, descended in part from Pietism. Pietist elements saturate modern Christianity, especially in America, in the form of anti-intellectualism—the distrust and neglect of the mind.

Everyone says balance is best, but not all agree on what balance is. The Pietists corrected an imbalance in their day but pushed the pendulum hard the other way. In the absence of theological reflection, an excess of emotion and "me-ism" arose and still grows. The pursuit of biblical truth must always be blended with a warm heart, but the mind should never be abandoned in the process.

The Scientific Revolution

Sir Isaac Newton invented neither the Fig Newton nor gravity, though he deciphered the latter. He wasn't the only scientist of faith, but we'll use him to represent others such as Galileo (astronomy), William Harvey (medicine), Robert Boyle (chemistry), and Antoni van Leeuwenhoek (microbiology). Such a star-studded list of believing scientists debunks the myth that Christianity and science oppose one another.

Newton was born near Lincolnshire, England, on Christmas Day in the year that Galileo died. Newton's own father had died before he was born, and his mother left him to grandparents while he was still a boy. Though raised on a farm, he fell in love with books. He enrolled at Cambridge to study theology, but physics and math captured his brilliant mind.

Newton wondered if the universe was an intricate machine, running according to preset rules. The symmetry he saw in nature, he reasoned, must have come from a Designer who imposed mathematical laws on what He made. By applying math to physics, Newton and others began unlocking the laws that run the world. His theory of gravity changed how the universe was understood, including how planets move. From his knowledge of optics, he figured out how rainbows form. He invented a telescope to collect light and a theory that explained the light.

Newton's creative mind even pondered the nature of God. For all his scientific discoveries, he ranked Scripture above science, and he hoped his theories would bring people to God. He wrote more than a million words about the Bible and theology—more than he wrote on science. But he hid a theological skeleton in his mental closet, namely his doubt about the doctrine of the Trinity.

His monumental *Mathematical Principles* (1687), blending the physics of motion into a single law of gravity, was notoriously hard to understand. But in his conclusion of the second edition, he inserted clear statements of theology, such as his belief that an infinite, eternal God rules all things, as seen in our solar system's perfect design.

Newton, along with philosopher René Descartes, jump-started the Enlightenment and shaped modern science until the twentieth century. Some Enlightenment thinkers drifted into the Deistic camp, believing in an impersonal God who abandoned the world after making it. Others discarded all belief in God. Newton retained his.

During the sixteenth and seventeenth centuries, the world reeled beneath two revolutions: one religious, the other scientific. Scholars debate the relationship between the two, but evidence suggests that Protestantism gave rise to modern science. Without belief in a personal God who designed an ordered universe, the scientific venture seems meaningless. But Christian thinkers of the time could see that the world operated by uniform laws that could be discovered.

The claim that science began from Christianity alone may be an overstatement, but the charge that Christianity and science are at war is pure myth. Even Sir Isaac Newton, the greatest scientist-mathematician of several centuries, believed in God and science at the same time.

The Birth of Modern Missions

Most eighteenth-century Christians thought the Great Commission applied only to the apostles' generation. The Moravians knew better and began spreading the gospel around the world. The modern missions movement began on October 8, 1732, when a Dutch ship carrying two Moravian missionaries sailed from Copenhagen, bound for the West Indies.

The Moravians were Pietists from a mostly German Lutheran background who traced their roots to Jan Hus. After his martyrdom, remnants of his movement called the Bohemian Brethren survived persecution by going underground. During the Reformation era, they spread across Europe before being nearly wiped out in the Thirty Years War. After they lived in Moravia, the Germans called them Moravians and the name stuck.

In 1722, while looking for a safe place to settle, they were invited to live on the estate of a young German Count named Nikolaus Ludwig von Zinzendorf. He welcomed other Pietist groups who sought asylum, and together they established a community called Herrnhut, with Zinzendorf as their leader. The young Count was eccentric—downright odd, according to some—and he never shed the snooty demeanor that came with his station in life. He was, after all, heir to one of Europe's elite families.

When Zinzendorf attended the coronation of King Christian VI in Copenhagen in 1731, he met two Eskimos from Greenland and a West Indian African—all converts to Christianity. They begged him to send missionaries to the slaves in the Indies. He shared their appeal with the Moravian community, who dispatched two men to the island of St. Thomas the next year.

Over the next thirty years the Moravians established mission outposts in Estonia, Greenland, Labrador, Surinam, South America, and several places in Africa as well as among the American Indians. They understood two missions principles that not all missionaries have grasped even today: (1) fit into the host culture, and (2) build spiritual self-sufficiency in the converts rather than make them dependent on Westerners.

John Wesley was influenced by Moravians he met while sailing from England to the American colony of Georgia. As their ship was pummeled by repeated storms, he feared dying, but the Moravians calmly sang hymns. He was so impressed that he visited Herrnhut a few months later. He liked most of what he saw there, but he was disturbed by the self-righteousness he observed as well as the personality cult surrounding the Count.

Over the next sixty years, these former religious refugees sent out three hundred missionaries. History records that the Herrnhut community started a round-the-clock prayer meeting in 1727 that went on nonstop for more than one hundred years. That sounds far-fetched, but even if it's close to being true, it may explain the Moravians' extraordinary missions success. They had their quirks, but if God selects a missions all-star team in heaven, at least a few Moravians will be on the squad.

America's Greatest Theologian

America's greatest theologian, and possibly its leading thinker of any category, was the Puritan pastor Jonathan Edwards. He was born in Connecticut in 1703, the son, grandson, and great-grandson of pastors. His father educated Edwards at an early age to prepare him as a young teen to enter Yale, where he received his first degree at seventeen and his master's degree at nineteen. He tutored at Yale before being called in 1727 to serve the church in Northampton, Massachusetts, under the pastorate of his famous grandfather, Solomon Stoddard. Two years later Stoddard died, and at the age of twenty-six Edwards assumed the pastorate of that influential church.

Edwards' preaching was so compelling that his people urged him to publish his sermons. His messages, preached in 1734–1735 and in 1740–1742, resulted in an extraordinary movement of the Spirit among his congregation and influenced a spiritual awakening across New England. But beginning in 1743 Edwards' relationship with his church turned sour, leading to his removal in 1750. The main complaint against him was that he would not allow into church membership those who claimed to be Christians but who lacked evidence of genuine conversion. Also, his preaching about fair treatment for Native Americans was not well received by all.

After being forced out of Northampton, Edwards became a missionary pastor to the Housatonic Indians at the frontier village of Stockbridge, Massachusetts. In that relative isolation he wrote his greatest works. In 1757 he accepted appointment as president of Princeton College, but shortly after his arrival he became ill and died from a smallpox inoculation.

Edwards preached God's Word clearly, argued it rationally, and insisted on living it daily. His tightly reasoned sermons riveted his hearers' attention. Despite the fact that he merely read his intellectually challenging messages from a manuscript in a monotone voice, those listening came under such conviction that they would sometimes react physically, such as crying out and grabbing the back of the pew in front of them. At times Edwards had to pause so that he would not be drowned out by the noise of his parishioners.

The picture of Edwards presented today is often

distorted to make him appear grim and stuffy. In reality, we may owe more to this man than to any other American Christian. He was a profound scholar with a God-fired heart, who allowed no divorce between deep scholarship and spiritual passion. He integrated intense faith and intellectual vigor, resulting in a Christian worldview for the New World and causing some to consider him the Augustine of North America.

He and his people weren't as stodgy as their image suggests. The first four of his children were born on Sunday, causing his people to tease him because the folklore of the day held that children were conceived on the day of the week on which they were born. Imagine a church full of stuffy Puritans teasing their pastor, the great Jonathan Edwards, about that!

For a lifetime Edwards worked tirelessly to understand, teach, and live the Bible. He believed that learning God's truth resulted in changed character on the inside and good works on the outside. He thought deeply, spoke plainly, and lived with vibrant passion for God, His Word, and His work.

America's Prerevolution

Colonial America rejected British rule on the heels of another revolution—a spiritual revolution called the Great Awakening. Between 1720 and the Revolutionary War, religious passion swelled in a series of waves that peaked about 1740. During that time, thousands came to faith through the preaching of God's Word. What led to that?

By the early 1700s, Americans no longer struggled to survive, and their spiritual passion had cooled. Commerce flourished, wealth spread, and acquisition of material goods increased. Going to church became a sign of social respectability more than a pursuit of truth, and most people avoided church entirely. Even pastors were more concerned with their preaching skills than with their sermons' content.

But God lit a fire in 1720 through Dutch Reformed preacher Theodore Frelinghuysen. He came to America from Germany and was stunned to see the spiritual apathy. Nevertheless, his preaching campaign in New Jersey reaped a huge harvest. The spiritual fire spread across the middle colonies and into the South, infecting Presbyterians, Methodists, and Baptists. It finally came to Congregationalists in New England and shook the world through George Whitefield and Jonathan Edwards.

The most popular figure was Whitefield, an itinerant preacher who could speak to thirty thousand people and be heard by all. Never before had America seen anything like this young British preacher. Crowds gathered out of nowhere as people raced for miles on horseback to hear of God's grace and Christ's death for sinners. His preaching throughout the colonies unified the movement into a singular whole, collectively called the Great Awakening.

But the uproar stirred the religious pot. While some clergy were thrilled, others were alarmed by reports of wild emotion and laypeople accusing pastors of spiritual deadness. Edwards wrote a cautious defense of the awakening, exposing his readers to what was happening in the soul. He also warned people about excessive emotion in response to flamboyant but shallow preaching. It might not stick, he said, once the excitement wears off. Continued exposure to God's Word was needed to prove such conversions were real.

During the Great Awakening, tens of thousands

came to Christ and 150 churches were started in New England alone. Denominational barriers were lowered, and evangelism and missions increased. Humanitarian efforts were started, and new colleges were founded to train pastors. The culture became more individualistic, paving the way for political independence. The most lasting effect came from Edwards' preaching of the doctrine of justification by faith and through his writings that describe the results of true conversion. In the process he established himself as America's premier theologian and helped start two later awakenings.

America needs another great awakening. Today's spiritual stupor may be severe, but God still breathes life into spiritually dead people and churches. His grace is best when needed most. May it come soon and last long.

Apostle to the Indians

Early relations between Europeans and American Indians fluctuated between civil and bloody. At times history has pictured the Indians as subhuman savages; at other times, white men have been portrayed as devils. Some real-life examples of those images do exist, but most people on both sides fell between the extremes. One great model of sacrifice was David Brainerd, Presbyterian missionary to the Indians, who gave his life to serve them.

A few Englishmen had already worked among the Indians. John Eliot and Thomas Mayhew Jr. and Sr. saw a few come to Christ in seventeenth-century Massachusetts. But not all white settlers approved, and the work died out. As a result of the Great Awakening, Indian missions resumed, and a few pastors, such as Jonathan Edwards, preached to the Indians. Brainerd's passion to reach them was also born in those revival times, which stimulated evangelism and missions in hundreds of American churches.

Brainerd was born in Haddam, Connecticut. He was

orphaned at fourteen and intended to farm his inherited land. But after his conversion at twenty-one, he attended Yale to prepare for ministry. The intensity that would serve him well as a missionary got him expelled from school. Perhaps too enthusiastic because of the Great Awakening, he took a dim view of one of his tutors and accused him of having no more grace than a chair. That remark earned him the heave-ho.

He continued his studies with a private tutor and was licensed to preach in 1742 by the association of ministers in Danbury, Connecticut. A mission society soon commissioned him to work among the Indians of western Massachusetts, Pennsylvania, and New Jersey. Having no further need of his inheritance, he gave it away to pay for a friend's education. During much of his missionary work, Brainerd lived like an Indian, sleeping in a wigwam and eating Indian food. At first he saw no results, but in time the Spirit worked, and in a one-year stretch, seventy-seven Indians came to Christ and continued in the faith.

Brainerd labored among the Indians for only four years. In 1746, while on an extended preaching tour along the Susquehanna River, his old tuberculosis worsened. He refused to stop, and this seriously damaged his health. Unable to continue his work for several months, he spent some of his recovery time in the home of his mentor, Jonathan Edwards. During this convalescence, he was nursed by Edwards' daughter Jerusha. They fell in love and became engaged, but Brainerd died before they could marry.

Brainerd left a diary describing his life on the frontier, which was edited and published by Edwards in 1749. His life was short, but his diary lived on, inspiring future missionaries, including William Carey, known as the father of modern missions. God gave Brainerd only twenty-nine years (the same as twentieth-century martyr Jim Elliot), but it was enough to make a difference forever.

However many years God gives each of us, we should make them count, as David Brainerd did. When we enter eternity, our opportunity to make a difference for Christ will be over. The length of life God gives is less important than the service we put into those years.

JOHN WESLEY (1703–1791)

Seeking Perfection

Two boys named John, born an ocean apart in 1703, would grow up to shake the world. They never met, but they admired the work God did through each other. One was Jonathan Edwards of New England, a major player in America's Great Awakening. The other, John Wesley in England, would become the key figure in Britain's revival during the same period.

Wesley's parents came from Puritan stock, and his father, Samuel, served as rector of the Anglican Church in Epworth. His extraordinary mother, Susanna, bore nineteen children (John was number 15), although several died young. When John was six, he escaped death when he was thrown from a second-story window into a neighbor's arms when the parsonage burned down. Susanna established a pattern in her children's lives by reading to them and teaching them the Bible. She even gave each child one-on-one training once a week. To find her own private space for reading and prayer, she had to pull her long dress over her head to shut out the children.

John and his brother Charles attended Oxford, where John read widely among the devotional classics and the early church Fathers. He and future evangelist George Whitefield were known for being mischievous, but they and Charles settled down and formed the Holy Club. Other students taunted the small group, calling them "Methodists" for seeking a method of spirituality. Their habits of Bible study, prayer, fasting, and service among the downtrodden formed the basis of a future, much wider movement.

In 1738 Wesley was convicted of his sinfulness but came to assurance of salvation while reading Luther's preface to Romans. After helping Whitefield in his work, Wesley began his own preaching ministry. When thousands responded, needing guidance in their new spiritual life, he organized helpers to meet the need. Wesley maintained a rigorous schedule, waking at 4:00 a.m. and never wasting a moment of time. The disciplined life allowed him to preach to the common people several times a day as he traveled England, Scotland, and Ireland on horseback up to sixty miles daily—a routine he kept into his seventies.

By the time he died at age eighty-eight, Wesley had traveled 250,000 miles and preached 40,000 sermons. Methodism had grown into a powerful denomination in

England and soon would do the same in America. He published his sermons, wrote the first religious tracts, and pioneered a monthly magazine. His brother Charles (1708–1788) left his mark too: He wrote about 6,500 hymns, many of them loved and sung today, such as "And Can It Be?" and "Hark the Herald Angels Sing."

Despite his parents' Puritan upbringing, Wesley's theology leaned toward Arminianism. His most noted distinctive was his doctrine of complete holiness. His views evolved over time, but he usually did not mean that total perfection could be attained in this life, at least as most people understand perfection. He believed that God's love can so transform the soul that sinless motives of the heart become natural.

Today evangelicalism bears the thumbprint of Wesley as well as of Edwards. Methodist churches claim about seventy million people, and Wesley's emphasis is found in holiness, Pentecostal, and charismatic groups, as well as Wesleyan colleges and seminaries.

The Greatest Evangelist?

Who was history's greatest evangelist? Billy Graham? Dwight Moody? No one knows, but we had better add George Whitefield (pronounced *witfield*) to the list of candidates. He was an eighteenth-century phenomenon with rock-star status. Long before high-tech mass media, he spoke face-to-face to 80 percent of the people in America. Even though British, he was the most famous person in America until George Washington. Twenty-three thousand came to hear his farewell sermon in Boston—more people than lived in the city at the time. Never before had America seen a crowd or a personality that large.

Whitefield was born at the Bell Inn in Gloucester and educated by his widowed mother. When he went to school, he did well, but he had to drop out at fifteen to go to work. At nineteen he enrolled at Oxford, where he met the Wesley brothers and joined their Holy Club. He was bright, though not scholarly, and no one could match his preaching.

The Anglican Church ordained him, but some

Anglicans later regretted it. Their preachers were stiff and proper; Whitefield was intense, passionate, even theatrical, yet spoke clearly and simply so all could understand. Not everyone liked that. When he wasn't allowed into Anglican pulpits, Whitefield preached in the fields to the common people, and they responded in huge numbers. Highbrow Anglicans feared it might cause commoners to riot, and some were horrified to hear themselves called sinners like the riffraff of the street.

Whitefield faced opposition for preaching outside to the masses (considered rabble-rousing by many Brits) and for preaching about sin and judgment, which is never popular. He received death threats and was shot at, attacked by mobs, and even stoned and left for dead. He once preached through a barrage of thrown rocks, eggs, and dead cats! But nothing stopped him. He preached his way across England, Ireland, Scotland, Holland, and Bermuda. He came to America seven times, preaching in all the colonies and striking the match that lit the Great Awakening. He preached at Harvard and four times in Jonathan Edwards' pulpit.

Whitefield began the day by preaching a 5:00 a.m. sermon. Most weeks he delivered a dozen sermons, totaling forty hours of speaking. He drove himself so

hard and preached with such intensity that he sometimes vomited blood after he finished. Keeping that pace
may have contributed to his death at only fifty-six. He
had given eighteen thousand Bible-soaked sermons,
addressing as many as ten million listeners. His old
friend John Wesley, who preached his funeral sermon,
said no one since the apostles had called so many sinners to repentance.

Whitefield introduced methods used in later awakenings. His most novel was open-air evangelism among
the masses. In the next century American Methodists
and Baptists took that idea and blazed across the frontier with it. Meanwhile, his biggest legacy, shared with
Wesley and Edwards, is evangelicalism itself. That mix
of Puritanism and Pietism blended the three giants' core
commitments: the authority of Scripture, individual
conversion by faith alone, personal devotion, and commitment to evangelism.

With due respect to God's faithful servants Graham
and Moody, Whitefield may have been history's greatest
evangelist. And while few of us may hope to equal those
three men in our impact on the world, all of God's people
share their mission: giving the gospel to the lost.

WILLIAM CAREY (1761–1834)

The Father of
Modern Missions

In the late eighteenth century Christianity resided mainly in Europe and North America. Most of the world had never heard the message of evangelical Protestantism. By the close of the nineteenth century, however, Christianity covered the globe, and this change was due largely to William Carey.

He was born in 1761 to a poor family near Northamptonshire, England. They had no money for education, but at the age of twelve, Carey taught himself Latin. At sixteen, about the time of his conversion, he became an apprentice cobbler. As he learned his new trade, he began to study the Bible.

Carey was consumed with learning and often fasted to save money for books. He accepted a call to pastor a Baptist church but still worked as a cobbler to make ends meet. He concluded from his study that the church was responsible to take the gospel to all people—a wild idea at the time. Most Christians believed that the Great

Commission applied only to the apostles' generation, so when Carey committed to go to India, his father, his wife, and people in his church thought he was nuts.

Before he left, Carey did two things that produced a huge impact. First, he gave one of the most influential sermons of all time: "Expect Great Things [from God]; Attempt Great Things [for God]." Second, he wrote a short book (eighty-seven pages) with a big title: *An Inquiry into the Obligation of Christians to Use Means for the Conversion of the Heathen* (and that's the short version of the title). Its influence has been compared to that of Luther's ninety-five theses.

Carey went to India, his resistant wife in tow. He first worked at Bengal, under the umbrella of the British East India Trading Company. But the trading company's workers were driven by making money, not saving souls, and proved a hindrance to Carey's work. So he moved to Serampore, under Dutch oversight, to work with a teacher and a printer who followed him to India. They made a powerful team, planting churches, learning the languages, translating and printing Bibles, founding colleges, and reforming the culture.

Carey eventually taught himself several of the local languages and published their grammars and lexicons. He oversaw the Bible's translation into six languages and parts of it into two dozen others. His linguistic genius could no longer be hidden, and he was appointed professor of Sanskrit, Bengali, and Marathi at Fort William College in Calcutta.

But he paid a high price for his service. The climate and conditions were hard; he wrestled with government bureaucracy; and he buried two wives and several of his children. Through it all, he never returned to England in forty-one years.

Carey pioneered modern missions ideas that we take for granted. He also tried to end the customs of infanticide and widow burning (cremating the wife of a dead man with his body). Even before Carey died, his example was elevating missions in the eyes of Christians everywhere. We see a recurrent theme in his life: God often prepares His servants by the discipline of hardship. By not quitting in tough times, Carey was used by God beyond anyone's expectations. The keys to his spiritual success were faith, determination, and persistence.

Social Reformer

Slavery still exists in parts of the world today, but a great blow was struck against it early in the nineteenth century by William Wilberforce and a group of his friends. This group was called the Clapham Sect because they often met in Clapham, just north of London, to pray, study the Bible, and draft political strategy. They knew that slavery violated Christianity, and they were determined to stop it.

By 1770 the British Empire was the world's greatest power. Its ships hauled more than half the annual cargo of a hundred thousand slaves from Africa. The empire's financial and political commitment to that horrible enterprise was colossal. So how could one small group make a difference? By one man's prayer-backed oratory before the world's most powerful body: the British Parliament.

Wilberforce was a child of wealth and privilege, but when he was eight, his father died. He was raised by an aunt whose home was frequented by the likes of George Whitefield, the great evangelist, and John Newton, the converted slave trader who wrote "Amazing Grace." At the age of fourteen, in a sign of things to come, Wilberforce wrote a letter to the editor of the local newspaper, attacking slavery.

He graduated from Cambridge at twenty and was elected to Parliament the next year. The big change in his life came at twenty-five, when he was converted after reading Philip Doddridge's book *The Rise and Progress of Religion in the Soul*. It fueled his lifelong campaign against slavery. His old friend John Newton, probably motivated by memories of his own slave-trading past, convinced Wilberforce to use his political influence in God's service.

Wilberforce gave his first antislavery speech to Parliament in 1789. When it led nowhere, he and his Clapham friends were convinced they needed more political clout. They began working at getting public opinion on their side, then bringing that opinion to bear on Parliament. Finally, in 1807, Wilberforce succeeded in getting Parliament to abolish the slave trade within the British Empire. He then tried to convince all of Europe to prohibit slavery, and at the Congress of Vienna in 1815, most European states agreed. In 1825 he retired after grooming a replacement, Thomas Buxton, who in 1833 drove a law through Parliament that abolished slavery itself. Wilberforce died four days later, his life's dream fulfilled, at least in principle.

Wilberforce and his Clapham Sect also founded societies to promote missions abroad, protect evangelists in Britain, translate the Bible, and ease the lives of workers. Wilberforce himself belonged to sixty-nine such societies. He knew his calling from God and shrewdly applied his wealth, brains, charm, and eloquence to influence political insiders, including his friend Prime Minister William Pitt.

The British honored William Wilberforce's work by burying him at Westminster Abbey and building a statue in his memory. The amount of social good set in motion by Wilberforce and his Clapham society exceeds our ability to measure. But it reminds us that even a small number of people, if truly committed, can change the world in a big way.

CHARLES SPURGEON (1834–1892)

The Prince of Preachers

Charles Spurgeon was born in Kelvedon, England, without the aristocratic privilege or contacts of Wilberforce. His father and grandfather were poor preachers. His mother delivered seventeen children, of whom nine died in infancy. Spurgeon spent most of his growing-up years in a remote farming village. To the end of his life, he felt more at home there than in London, where he preached to thousands.

Lack of formal education didn't hold Spurgeon back. He had an amazing mind, and he valued learning. When he was only six, he read *Pilgrim's Progress* and loved it so much that he eventually read it more than a hundred times. His library contained twelve thousand volumes, and he read six books per week. His mentors were the Puritans, whose writings he devoured as a teenager. Their deep theology, intense spirituality, and practical application shaped his soul and ministry.

Spurgeon began preaching as a teen, and his gifts showed. At seventeen he became pastor of a rural Baptist church, and two years later, pastor of New Park

71 | MISSIONS MOMENTUM (1789–1900)

Street Church in London. That congregation of two hundred grew to six thousand during his thirty-eight-year tenure. Members of the royal family and Parliament, Prime Minister Gladstone, future U.S. President James Garfield, and other notables among the rich and famous came to hear him.

Spurgeon didn't claim to be a theologian, but his theology was thorough and thoroughly biblical. He was a Calvinist, but when he couldn't reconcile divine election and human responsibility, he accepted both because Scripture taught both. He lived and preached when liberal theology was invading Europe's pulpits from German universities. When he feared that other conservative Baptist preachers were abandoning core Christian doctrines, he withdrew from his Baptist Union.

Spurgeon preached up to ten times per week. His sermons were instructive and yet evangelistic— dramatic, direct, compelling, and practical—and reminded old-timers of the Puritans, blending historic doctrine with up-to-date delivery. Over his lifetime, ten million people heard him, and his sermons were collected and published in sixty-three volumes, the largest work by any Christian author in history. His *All of Grace* was the first book published by Moody Press and remains its all-time bestseller. Sales of that and two of his other books exceed a million copies.

Spurgeon enjoyed laughter but suffered from depression; the responsibility for so many souls weighed on his heart. And like many who speak for God, he had his critics, adding to his heavy load. Over the last third of his life, he gained weight and suffered from gout and rheumatism. When he died, his body lay in state for three days at his Metropolitan Tabernacle while sixty thousand mourners passed by. A two-mile-long funeral parade followed Spurgeon's hearse; one hundred thousand people lined the streets; businesses closed and flags were lowered to half-mast.

His influence extended beyond preaching. His church gave money and started ministries to meet the needs of the urban poor. Spurgeon was especially fond of his Stockwell Orphanage. He also founded the Pastor's College, which trained nine hundred pastors during his lifetime. Twenty-five editions of his weekly sermons were sold in twenty languages; they were still being published a quarter-century after he died.

None of us today is going to be quite the same as Charles Spurgeon. But regardless of our gifts, talents, or training, we can stay true to God's Word and His call on our lives.

Escaping the Cannibals' Pot

One season of the television reality show *Survivor* was filmed on Vanuatu, a chain of South Pacific islands, formerly called the New Hebrides, located a thousand miles north of New Zealand. Today many of the native population are Christians, converted from their heritage of cannibalism. How did that happen? Ultimately, by God's empowering grace, but He used a tough, courageous missionary named John Paton.

Paton was born to a poor Presbyterian family in Dumfries, Scotland. His father fed his family by knitting stockings, and John quit school at eleven to help. He later wrote how his father led the family in devotions every morning and evening and made sure all eleven kids were in church on Sunday. That Christian heritage prepared Paton to risk his life to serve his Lord.

Paton first worked for the Glasgow City Mission, knocking on doors in the slums to share the gospel. He encountered threats and assaults—perfect training for the "reality show" he would later face among cannibals. After ten years of slum work, someone told him of South

Pacific islanders dying without ever hearing of Christ. He determined to go despite warnings that, just twenty years earlier, missionaries John Williams and James Harris had been eaten by those cannibals.

But Paton and his new bride, Mary Ann, sailed for the South Pacific in April of 1858, arriving on the island of Tanna in November. After a son was born to them on February 12, Mary Ann died on March 3. The baby, named after Paton's beloved father, died seventeen days later. Awash in his tears, and praying for strength, the missionary buried both loved ones with his own hands. He confessed in his biography that without the Lord he would have gone mad and died of grief.

Alone and lonely, Paton stayed on, going from village to village to share the love of God in Christ. He miraculously dodged repeated attempts on his life and was spared the ravages of disease, which wiped out a third of the island population. After nationals stole his supplies, he avoided starvation by fleeing to a missionary compound across the island. When his pursuers tried to kill him by burning down the house he was staying in, he escaped by ship.

Paton then toured Australia and Britain, raising money and recruiting missionaries. He remarried, to Margaret Whitecross, and returned to the New Hebrides, this time to the island of Aniwa, where people were more responsive to the gospel. The Patons remained for decades, planting a church, starting schools, building orphanages, and translating the Bible.

When he grew too old to continue in the bush, Paton resumed his speaking tours across Australia, Britain, and North America to arouse missions awareness. By the end of their work, the Patons' school had trained three hundred national evangelists, who took the gospel to all the islands of the New Hebrides, and two dozen missionary couples were working there with three of John and Margaret's ten children.

John Paton was a tough guy, tough enough to pay any price to reach the lost for Christ. Toughness is less physical than mental—the will to endure under pressure. We get it by being exposed to God's Word, then applying the Word to the hardships of life. As parents, we should be training our kids to be tough, and as individuals, we need to toughen up our own souls. The hardships of life, and faithfulness in God's service, require it.

DWIGHT MOODY (1837–1899)

"Crazy Moody"

God uses uneducated country boys as well as great scholars. A century ago, one of those rubes became as famous as Billy Graham is today.

Dwight Moody was one of nine children born to a Unitarian family near Northfield, Massachusetts. Family finances took a bad turn after Moody's father died when he was only four. As a result, his education ended at the fifth grade.

When Moody was seventeen, his uncle in Boston gave him a job in his shoe shop on the condition that Moody attend church. His Sunday school teacher led him to Christ, but he was refused church membership because he knew so little doctrine. Because of his lack of education and rural background, he came across as a bumpkin, but he had a knack for coming up with new ideas and making them work.

In 1856 Moody moved to Chicago and became a successful shoe salesman. He started a Sunday school for slum kids, financed by selling stocks. The idea worked, and before long, hundreds of kids were coming. Two years later Moody quit his job to give himself solely to ministry. In 1863, at age twenty-six, he became president of the Chicago Young Men's Christian Association (YMCA) and converted his Sunday school into a full-fledged church, later renamed the Moody Memorial Church. His energy and innovative methods were, by this time, so well known across Chicago that he was called Crazy Moody.

Moody's YMCA contacts earned him invitations to speak in Britain. His fame spread as he preached to crowds of up to twenty thousand. During his five-month London campaign, he preached to 2.5 million people. He returned to America a hero and held similar revivals with the same results. At the end of his second British tour, his farewell message in Glasgow, Scotland, attracted so many that he preached to forty thousand people outside the Great Crystal Palace because they couldn't find seats inside. At the 1893 Chicago World's Fair, he spoke to 130,000 in one day.

Unlike the ministries of many revivalists of the time, Moody's included more than evangelism. Perhaps motivated by his own lack of education, he started three schools, including one that was renamed Moody Bible Institute after he died. Two publishing houses originated from his work: Revell and Moody Press. He also established the annual Northfield Conferences, from which grew the Student Volunteer Movement for world missions. By 1920 it had sent out more than eight thousand foreign missionaries.

Moody's theology was bare bones, highlighting the three Rs: Ruined by the Fall, Redeemed by the blood, Regenerated by the Spirit. As a speaker, he was neither dramatic nor polished; just a country boy who engaged his audience with sentimental down-home stories. Moody died a few days before the nineteenth century closed, after God had used him to present the gospel to one hundred million people.

Dwight Moody was a wonderful servant of God. But his work, without his intending it, added to a gradual transition in the culture of American Christianity, changing it from a theology-grounded faith to an emotion-based event. We see the long-term result in our day. Feelings rather than doctrine rule the roost in American Christianity.

Becoming Chinese to Reach the Chinese

We all like warm, fuzzy personalities. Some people even rate charisma over character. Hudson Taylor had little charisma but lots of character.

Before he was born, Taylor's parents prayed for a son to do God's work in China, and at age four he was telling people he would do it. At seventeen, however, his passion for China was swamped by teenage rebellion. But he responded to the gospel message he read in a tract, and his vision for China returned. He began medical training the next year.

Taylor joined the Chinese Evangelization Society in 1853 and sailed for Shanghai. When he arrived, he discovered that many missionaries lived like royalty, cloistered within lavish, Western compounds, out of touch with the Chinese people. He made a commitment to live like the Chinese, and he traded his Western clothes for local dress, even shaving his head except for a braided pigtail. Other missionaries criticized him from the safety of their coastal cities as he penetrated the interior to pass out Bibles in villages.

Taylor's missions agency proved so inept that he resigned in 1857 and decided to go independent, trusting God to provide for his needs. The next year he married Maria Dyer, a missionary teacher who shared his passion for China. By 1860 they had planted a church in Ningpo and grown it to twenty-one members. But disease forced the Taylors to return to England the next year.

While in England, he finished his medical training and started the China Inland Mission (CIM) to take the gospel to every province of China. He was determined never to ask for money, just to pray and trust God to provide. Instead of resting, He worked at a furious pace, translating the Bible and recruiting missionaries by telling churches that "a million a month die without God." Despite continuing criticism and his own gruff manner, Taylor's recruiting campaign was wildly successful. He found and sent missionaries to all of China's eighteen provinces.

In 1866 he and Maria and sixteen other missionaries sailed from London, determined to evangelize inland China despite the cost. That cost proved high: Maria died at age thirty-three, and four of their children died before age ten. Taylor then married Jennie Faulding, who served with him for the rest of his life. In 1900, while he was in Switzerland, the Boxer Rebellion broke out, leading to the deaths of 135 missionaries and 53 of their children, many of them CIM people. Taylor was seventy and ill; he never fully recovered, although he lived five more years.

Taylor's greatest impact may have been in recruiting. His blunt, uncharismatic style attracted the right kind of people for such hard work. Wherever he spoke, young people lined up to go to China, and CIM became the largest missions agency in China. Taylor considered life an adventure of trusting God, and he influenced China for Christ as had no one before him. His bouts of depression, his prickly personality, and his demanding nature did not prevent God from using him in a unique way.

Charm and charisma are wonderful traits, but character trumps both. God used Hudson Taylor's strong-headed focus to change China, and today God still looks for people of faith, drive, and focus who will apply their singleness of purpose to His great plan.

Where Does Authority Lie?

Most Protestant/Catholic disputes boil down to a question of authority. Where does final authority lie—in Scripture alone or in Scripture as interpreted by tradition and the pope? Many Catholics consider the pope to be infallible (a word conservative Protestants apply only to Scripture). How and when did the Catholic doctrine of papal infallibility arise? Many Protestants think that Catholics have always believed the pope was infallible, but he wasn't officially given that status until July 13, 1870.

In the late eighteenth and early nineteenth centuries, the French Revolution and Napoleon's campaigns made a mess of Europe. Some Catholics thought the only way to restore order was by strengthening the papacy. The pope's infallibility was already assumed by most Catholics, but they thought that if it were made official, he could protect them from chaos and tyranny. Some Catholics were so desperate for a stronger Rome that they wrote hymns to Pope Pius IX (1792–1878) and called him the voice God.

Pius served longer than any previous pope, from 1846 to 1878. In 1854, without consulting bishops or councils, he proclaimed that Mary was conceived without original sin, an event called the Immaculate Conception. (That doctrine does not refer to Jesus' virgin birth, as many Protestants assume, but to Mary's sinlessness.) Some Catholics questioned whether the pope could establish doctrines on his own.

In 1864 Pius issued a Syllabus of Errors condemning modern, liberal trends such as popular democracy, freedom of conscience, religious toleration, and separation of church and state. Catholics disagreed among themselves over those issues, but the pope thought these were evils that threatened Rome. During his tenure, the Roman Church had lost much of its political power, so he was determined to enhance its religious authority.

Thinking the time was right to strengthen his hand, Pius called for the first general council since Trent in the sixteenth century. A total of 793 delegates, almost all from the papal stronghold of Europe, especially Italy, met in several sessions between December 8, 1869, and September 1, 1870. Six proposals were scheduled for discussion, but only two were actually addressed: one about the relationship between reason and revelation, and the other—the sticky one—about papal authority.

The council affirmed the decisions of Trent as well as the pope's Syllabus of Errors. It proclaimed that revelation was superior to reason and that revelation was found only in the Roman Catholic Church. It then declared that the pope, as Peter's successor, is the final authority in all matters of faith and practice when he speaks *ex cathedra,* that is, when he speaks officially as the pope. His formal pronouncements cannot be changed or overturned, do not require assent from bishops, and must be obeyed by the faithful. In 1954 Pope Pius XI used this authority to pronounce that Mary ascended bodily into heaven.

How one answers the question of authority determines the path taken in the search for truth. If truth is found in church tradition led by papal authority, we move down one path. If it's found only in God's revelation in Scripture, we proceed in a different direction. When authority is transferred away from the Bible, control is taken from God and given to people. Those who believe authority is in the Bible should be consistent with their view and study and obey it.

The Patron Saint of Baptist Missions

When Lottie Moon died, the *Foreign Missions Journal* called her "the best man among our missionaries." That statement wouldn't be well received today, but in 1912 it was a big compliment. She was ahead of her time, an amazing missionary who left her mark on China during her lifetime and still influences our world today.

Moon was born to an aristocratic Virginia family in 1840 and grew up on a plantation near the homes of presidents Jefferson, Madison, and Monroe. As a child, she was labeled "a devil" because of her defiant attitude, but she was given the education and culture befitting a Southern belle. Her fiercely independent mother, who was widowed when Moon was thirteen, molded her into the stuff of a tough cross-cultural missionary.

In college Moon rebelled against her Baptist upbringing, but her life turned around at a campus revival, and she dedicated herself to God's work. In 1861 she earned a master's degree in classics, going on to teach in Cartersville, Georgia, when the Civil War ended. But she dreamed of adventure and prepared to go to China as a missionary.

Moon arrived in northern China in 1873 and began teaching in a girls' school. When she found the students unmotivated and the work unfulfilling, she asked her field director to move her to evangelism and church planting. They clashed over that idea, so she went on her own to P'ing-tu to start a church. It was slow, hard work, but the people's willingness to learn drove her on.

In time she trained one of her converts, Li Shou Ting, to be the pastor, and over the next twenty years he baptized more than a thousand people. Southern Baptists called P'ing-tu their greatest evangelistic center in China. From 1890 to 1912, Moon alternated between doing evangelistic work in villages and training missionaries in Tengchow. And she wrote to Baptists back in America, appealing for missions support.

In the first decade of the twentieth century, northern China was ravaged by disease and famine. Moon organized relief efforts, but they proved inadequate for the widespread devastation. She even depleted her own bank account in trying to relieve the misery of the starving Chinese. After slipping into depression, she stopped eating and died of starvation on Christmas Eve 1912.

Moon gave her life for China, but like many missionaries, who usually serve in the hidden corners of the earth, her biggest impact came after she died. Her appeals for financial support for foreign missions resulted in the Southern Baptists' Women's Missionary Union. Their Christmas offering, which she started in 1888, now receives tens of millions of dollars each year. Over a billion dollars has been given to it.

Many women now do missions work and no one gives it a second thought. But in the nineteenth century that was revolutionary—and a little improper in some people's eyes. Lottie Moon was not deterred; she wanted China for Christ, and she gave her life in the process. The light of her determined and sacrificial spirit still shines, showing the way to serve Christ wherever we live.

Queen of the Calabar

God often converts a hard life into extraordinary service. Mary Slessor was born into poverty in Scotland in 1848. She grew up in a one-room apartment without water, lights, or plumbing. When her alcoholic father came home drunk, he would often kick her out of the house for the night. To help support the family, she starting working in the mills at age eleven, and from the time she was fourteen she provided most of the family's income by working ten-hour days.

When Slessor was still a child, she was led to Christ by a neighbor and began attending a nearby Presbyterian church. By her early twenties, after several years of service in that church, she "graduated" to mission work in the slums of Dundee. Facing down disruptive street gangs who hindered her work prepared her for future ministry.

Inspired by the life and death of David Livingstone, Slessor joined the Calabar Mission and sailed for Africa. The atrocities of slavery were still fresh when she landed on Nigeria's coast in 1876. She learned the local language

77

MISSIONS MOMENTUM
(1789–1900)

and began teaching. Africa was so dangerous that most missionary men worked from inside secure compounds, but she wanted to go inland to do pioneer missions work. After three years, though, malaria forced her home to Scotland on furlough.

When Slessor went back to Africa, she penetrated the interior, abandoned her European customs of food and clothing, and lived in a mud hut like the Africans. She supervised their educational efforts, judged their arguments, adopted abandoned children, and evangelized villages, all while opposing the witchcraft of area tribes. But she again grew so sick that she had to return to Scotland for medical care.

On her next trip to Africa, Slessor pushed further inland to places considered suicidal even for men. When she learned that her mother and two sisters had died, she felt released to enter the deepest jungles because no family members were left to worry about her. For twenty-five years she lived in a rat- and bug-infested mud hut, enduring terrible conditions resulting in boils on her face and head. At fifty-five Slessor and the seven abandoned children she had adopted moved to an even more remote area to begin another work. In addition to pursuing conventional ministries, she opposed brutal practices of the region such as the presumed right of men to kill women whenever they wished.

In 1915, after forty years of serving the Lord in Africa, Slessor died in her mud hut, leaving her adopted children to carry on her work. She had earned the respect of the British and the love of the Africans, who called her "mother of all the peoples." Her childhood poverty and difficulties had prepared her to endure Africa's hardships as few other Westerners could have done.

The life of Mary Slessor, "queen of the Calabar," teaches us that the tough times we face now may be God's training for greater service later. Rather than complain about what we perceive as misery, we should consider life's difficulties to be part of God's plan to prepare us for His work.

It All Belongs to Christ

"There is not a square inch in the whole domain of our human existence over which Christ, who is Sovereign over all, does not cry: 'Mine!'" So said Abraham Kuyper, Dutch Reformed pastor, theologian, educator, journalist, and statesman. He was born in Maassluis, the Netherlands, the son of the pastor of a Reformed church. After taking his undergraduate and doctoral degrees in theology at Leyden University, he himself served as a Reformed pastor.

Kuyper understood the central issue facing the church of his day. It was engaged in a fight to the death between two all-consuming worldviews: one based on humankind, its knowledge, and its abilities; the other submitted to Christ alone. Because both systems, secularism and Christianity, claimed sovereignty over all that is, no compromise was possible. His logic was irrefutable: If Christ is the sovereign Lord of the universe, then every sphere of society, culture, and thinking is His and should be brought under His reign.

Kuyper applied his profound intellect and deep piety

to this titanic clash of worldviews, calling on Christians to join him. He was the driving force behind the Dutch neo-Calvinist movement which tried to reshape the country based on Christian truth. Over his long, distinguished career, this multitalented man founded the Free University of Amsterdam, a newspaper, a labor union, and a political party—the first Christian Democratic Party in the world. He even served as prime minister of the Netherlands from 1901 to 1905.

Kuyper believed that every worldview begins with presuppositions, a set of assumptions accepted by faith. Every culture, text, and movement is based on a worldview that can be analyzed. One can then push it to its logical extreme to reveal its validity or disclose its errors.

Kuyper left his footprints across the worlds of theology, education, and politics, resulting in a renaissance of Calvinism in Holland. His influence came to North America when he gave the 1898 Stone Lectures at Princeton Seminary. In the twentieth century his ideas were developed by Herman Dooyeweerd in Europe and by Cornelius Van Til in America. Perhaps the most recognized name among those influenced by Kuyper's thinking is that of Francis Schaeffer, who introduced millions of Christians to worldview awareness and cultural analysis.

Kuyper's is not a household name, but he introduced a way of thinking that greatly affects us today. He could see what happens to a society when it trades one worldview for another, such as replacing Christianity with secularism. Many Christians deplore what's become of America and Europe, but Kuyper saw it coming a century ago and tried to do something about it.

Despite evangelical numbers, money, and political power in America, we have lost the culture. Our lack of worldview awareness is one reason why. Yet, like Abraham Kuyper, we can try to understand worldviews and discern their consequences for our culture. And then, also like Kuyper, we can act more wisely for Christ.

"Foreign Devils"

Respect for nationals and their culture plays a big part in the acceptance of missionaries in foreign lands. Most missionaries and government officials understand that today, but not all did in China in the nineteenth century. The result was the Boxer Rebellion, an effort by Chinese patriots to remove foreigners from China at the turn of the previous century.

From the 1840s, Western powers and Japan had carved up China as though by right, and unequal treaties were forced on China. Some foreigners hated and abused the Chinese people, and they were immune from prosecution because they enjoyed diplomatic privilege. A few missionaries were little more than the religious wing of their governments back home. Some publicly ridiculed Chinese beliefs and culture. As Western mistreatment and influence spread, the Chinese people grew increasingly frustrated, and foreigners were seen as devils.

The backlash was led by members of a quasi-secret group, the Society of Harmonious Fists, better known as the Boxers. To inflame people's hatred of foreigners, they passed out handbills that included false rumors of atrocities committed by missionaries. Because of their martial arts training and mystical superstitions, they believed they couldn't be killed by modern weapons. In the 1890s they accepted into their group thousands of refugees escaping the natural disasters that had struck northern China. Finally, in 1899, tensions peaked and violence erupted.

In January of 1900 the government in Peking (Beijing) encouraged the Boxers. The violence increased and some Chinese Christians were murdered. The big explosion came in June when several Western missionaries were killed and their buildings were burned. International troops arrived to try to restore the peace. But when they captured some Chinese forts, the empress dowager considered it a declaration of war and ordered foreigners to be killed and Christianity to be eradicated. Whatever restraint had been exercised before was gone, and the massacre began.

Madness reigned. Thousands of enraged Chinese destroyed churches, schools, hospitals, and orphanages. Some fifty thousand Chinese Christians were slaughtered. Western missionaries who couldn't escape were murdered. The heads of decapitated Christians were given as gifts to governors and displayed in public. Westerners who could reach their embassies in Peking sought refuge there. Finally, on August 14, troops from several countries arrived, and peace was restored.

The Boxer Rebellion delivered the worst blow to the modern missions movement. But it also inspired thousands of Western Christians to give their lives to missions, especially in China. The church within China experienced explosive growth as a result of the courage displayed by Chinese and Western Christians facing martyrdom. Tertullian was proved right again: "The blood of the martyrs is the seed of the church."

The church flourished in China for fifty years, until the advent of Communism shut it down again. Today, after half a century of atheistic, Communist rule, China is cautiously opening to Western ideas. Unadmitted by the government, tens of millions of Chinese have become Christians. The legacy of martyred saints, Chinese and Western alike, lives on.

From the West to the World

During the nineteenth century, world missions exploded. The global Christian population increased from less than 25 percent to almost 35 percent in a hundred years. The church hadn't grown that rapidly since the fourth century. By the early 1900s, forty-five thousand missionaries were working in the field, and the prospect of "reaching the world in this generation" seemed close enough to touch.

But more than half the people on earth still hadn't heard the gospel. Much work remained to be done. And despite the great international success, new forces threatened the church in Europe and America, the home base for most missionaries. Secularization without and liberalism within were driving millions of Europeans and Americans out of the church.

The first International Missions Conference assembled in Edinburgh, Scotland, in 1910 to survey the situation and build cooperation. Christianity had spread far and fast, but the church was led by Europeans and Americans wherever it went. It covered the globe but was not truly global. A total of 160 mission societies sent thirteen hundred delegates to the conference, almost all from countries that had colonized the world. Only a handful came from Asia and none from Latin America.

The ten-day event was filled with promising speeches. Optimism soared in the atmosphere of unity. Many spoke of the need to form indigenous churches. But not all agreed; some attendees equated being Christian with being Western. The two main results of the conference were (1) a sense of unity that eventually led toward ecumenism and the formation of the World Council of Churches in 1948 and (2) an awareness among most delegates that Christianity was international and therefore the church should become more indigenous. The conference marked a transition of ages; the era of colonial missions was drawing to a close as an age of global cooperation was dawning. Throughout the twentieth century, the church would become less Western and more varied in its expressions of Christianity.

The conference also visited some of the liberal ideas from German universities, like whether Christianity was God's final revelation or simply His best revelation. Leaders of mainline denominations were intrigued by these new ideas, and the more they accepted them in the coming years, the more their passion for missions declined. Within a generation, liberal theology all but killed biblical Christianity in Europe and seriously threatened the church in America.

We learn diverse lessons from the International Missions Conference of 1910 and its aftermath. First, Christians from multiple denominations and backgrounds can cooperate on the mission field. But if we sacrifice essential Christian doctrines, we've lost Christianity and are left with only generic, universal religion. Second, we must develop national leaders instead of perpetuate Western culture throughout the church in non-Western lands. The theological insights of the Reformation in Europe and then America surpass any in history. But unchanging truth will be expressed in different forms as Christianity spreads to various countries and cultures.

Most missionaries have learned these lessons, leading to an explosion of nonwhite, non-European Christianity. Jesus Christ is now praised by people in nearly every part of the globe, and today the greatest vitality of God's church lies in Africa, Asia, and South America.

The Baseball Player Evangelist

In the 1820s and 1830s Charles Finney (1792–1875) introduced new measures into revivalism. He appeared to depend more on human resources than on God's, and he learned that organization and theatrics could increase the numbers who responded. Almost a century later, Billy Sunday was one of the best at it.

Sunday was born to a poor farm family near Ames, Iowa. He received little schooling, and his only theological training came from YMCA Bible classes. As a great athlete, he began a big-league baseball career in 1883, playing for Chicago, Pittsburgh, and Philadelphia. Between games and while traveling, he learned the life and lingo of urban saloons and theaters.

While playing for the Chicago White Stockings in 1886, Sunday visited the Pacific Garden Mission, heard the gospel, and "got saved." For the next few years, he still played baseball and gave motivational talks for the YMCA, but in 1891 he left the game for full-time ministry. The $5,000 yearly salary he gave up may not sound like much today, but it was then. He traded it for a $75 monthly salary with the YMCA.

In 1893 Sunday became the advance man for evangelist Walter Chapman. When Chapman accepted a pastorate two years later, Sunday began his own evangelistic career. He worked the small towns of the Upper Midwest, but when World War I broke out, he took his revival tent and sawdust trail to Chicago, Boston, and New York. His urban street-smarts and intense patriotism were perfect for the big cities in wartime.

Sunday was a showman—as much actor as preacher. His flamboyant style could match that of any vaudeville performer. He played up his hick background, calling himself a rube, and the crowds loved it. His folksy language, earthy descriptions, and acrobatic gestures often brought applause from the audience. Sunday was the greatest show in town, and the press spread his fame.

Then came the roaring twenties. The war was over, and Sunday's antibooze pitch was less appealing. Invitations to preach dried up as religious entertainment went out of vogue. He spent his final years working the small Midwestern towns where he had begun.

Sunday preached to tens of millions of people in two hundred campaigns. He claimed to have won almost

100,000 people to Christ in New York in 1917 alone. In some small towns, 20 percent of the people allegedly came to Christ. But even in that age, when intense emotion was often taken as a sign of conversion, people wondered how many of Sunday's converts were genuine. God surely used the gospel Sunday preached, but many were counted merely for marching in his patriotic, anti-booze parades or passing through the line to shake his hand. After the show ended and the emotion faded, few joined a church or changed their lives.

Some Christians still think the spiritual summit is walking the aisle in a dramatic display of "getting saved." But salvation is not the end, only the beginning. That's why Jesus called it new *birth*. Birth is the beginning, to be followed by a lifetime of growth. We might do well to consider what conversion is and what evidence of it we should see. We might also be more thoughtful and thorough in explaining the gospel and its implications. Entertainment and emotion can't replace God's truth or the Spirit's work.

Drifting to Extremes

By the turn of the twentieth century, modernism gave skeptics reason to doubt Christianity, or so it seemed. Christ's deity and virgin birth, humanity's fallen nature and need of salvation, Jesus' substitutionary death and subsequent resurrection, and especially the Bible's inspiration and reliability were under attack. These doctrines were replaced by an optimistic view of the human race as able to save itself—an idea stemming from evolution applied to religion.

Liberal theology originated in German universities a century before 1920, and Americans who studied in Europe brought it home with them. True religion, according to liberal thinking, wasn't found in a book but in our feelings of dependence on God. Theology therefore didn't focus on the Bible's statements but rather on one's experience of the Almighty. The highest application of these insights was social ethics for the common good, called "love." Thus the kingdom of God would be realized on earth. In response to the growing liberal threat, conservatives published a series of booklets called *The Fundamentals* between 1910 and 1915 to defend core Christian beliefs.

The explosion occurred in Dayton, Tennessee, during the 1925 Scopes Monkey trial. High school science teacher John Scopes had taught evolution in defiance of a state law prohibiting such teaching. He was convicted, but the trial was turned into a circus by the hostile Eastern media, who portrayed believers of Creation and Christianity as ignorant, bigoted hillbillies. The Broadway play *Inherit the Wind* and two movies based on it spread that impression across the country, and it persists in some circles today.

Liberals benefited from the debacle as colleges, seminaries, and churches drifted their way. Fundamentalists started their own institutions and largely abandoned the culture to the forces of liberalism. As liberals took over seminaries and pulpits, fundamentalists responded with a militant, separatist view toward all of life, especially the life of the mind. Anti-intellectualism flourished in their run-and-hide world. Education and the intellect were considered dangerous, even un-Christian. Emotion and experience were valued above thinking.

But liberalism was struck a blow by the Depression and two world wars. If human nature is basically good, and if society is improving in an upward evolutionary spiral, where did such massive suffering come from? Liberal thinking was caught flat-footed, unprepared to respond to such horrific evils. Human depravity and our need of help from outside ourselves were all too apparent. Although certain liberal doctrines continued, classic liberalism as a system was over.

Fundamentalism survived but was loaded down with serious baggage. Public perception hadn't changed since the Scopes trial, and fundamentalism's anti-everything, separatist stance was suicidal. Finally, in the late 1940s, conservatives such as Carl Henry and Billy Graham presented a more mellow form of conservative Christianity without compromising core doctrines, and modern evangelicalism was born.

Evangelicals value the mind and believe God calls Christians to engage the culture rather than run from it. As such, evangelicalism now enjoys a far wider social acceptance than fundamentalism ever did. But that popularity may pose a threat. To maintain its popularity, will evangelicalism either loosen its hold on biblical doctrine or cease to prophetically challenge the culture where it is at fault? Christians must ever renew their commitment to lovingly penetrate and influence society with God's truth.

J. GRESHAM MACHEN (1881–1937)

A Nonfundamentalist Fundamentalist

"False ideas are the greatest obstacles to the reception of the gospel." So warned J. Gresham Machen at the start of the modernist/fundamentalist debate. He urged Christians not to retreat from the intellectual war, but most Christians did anyway. And as conservatives stopped learning and thinking, liberal forces took over America's universities and pulpits. Machen was the leading spokesman for fundamentalism, although he was not strictly a fundamentalist himself. He adhered to most of the fundamentalists' theology, but he was too scholarly to embrace their narrow anti-intellectualism and legalistic tendencies.

Machen was born to a prominent Baltimore lawyer and reared in a cultured home. His father loved the classics and rare books; his mother, Victorian literature. Machen received his BA in classics from Baltimore's Johns Hopkins University in 1901. He then did a year of graduate studies at Johns Hopkins, followed by simultaneously taking two graduate degrees, an MA in philosophy at Princeton University and a BD at Princeton Seminary. His professors saw his promise and urged him to pursue advanced studies in Europe. During his year in Germany—one semester at Marburg and another at Göttingen—he found himself at the center of the higher critical studies that attacked the Bible.

Upon returning from Europe, Machen began his teaching career as professor of New Testament at Princeton. In 1921 Princeton Seminary's great scholar and spokesman, B. B. Warfield, died and the leadership of conservatism at Princeton fell into Machen's hands. By the end of the decade, the liberal side held the upper hand and Machen came under fire from both the seminary and his denomination, the Presbyterian Church in the USA (PCUSA). In 1929 he and supportive faculty left Princeton to found Westminster Seminary in Philadelphia.

After Machen formed a new missions board to prevent liberalism among Presbyterian missionaries, his denomination suspended him from ministry in 1935. He and friends left the PCUSA and formed the Presbyterian Church in America (PCA), later renamed the Orthodox Presbyterian Church (OPC). (Today's PCA was started a generation later.) On New Year's Day 1937, while on a trip to Bismark, North Dakota, to gather support for his new denomination, he died of pneumonia.

Machen's writings were widely read by both scholarly and popular audiences. His liberal adversaries couldn't dismiss him as they did other conservatives; his arguments were too thoughtful and logical to be ignored. His attack on liberalism struck at the heart. He said that liberalism wasn't an updated version of Christianity at all but rather a whole new religion that placed faith in humankind while using Christian vocabulary to promote its novel ideas. It was only thinly disguised Unitarianism (an anti-trinitarian religion that denies the deity of Christ), and he challenged liberals to be honest enough to admit it.

J. Gresham Machen was a scholar's scholar who stood his ground for God's truth under withering assaults from his enemies, and he paid a heavy price for it. In a theological world dominated by liberal scholars and anti-intellectual fundamentalists, he fought for the truth without abandoning his faith or his intellect. In the process, he demonstrated that a scholar at the highest level can believe orthodox Christian doctrines. His example reminds us that all Christians can study hard, think well, and defend the faith to the best of our God-given ability. Meanwhile, churches can be looking for promising scholars to train and support.

The Neoorthodox Champ

No one likes to stand alone against the crowd, especially if that crowd includes both friends and enemies. Swiss theologian Karl Barth faced that challenge when confronted with Germany's liberal theology and Hitler's Nazi Party.

By the early twentieth century, Europe lay beneath a tidal wave of liberal doctrine. But Barth stopped the flood and started a revolution in theology, later called neoorthodoxy. He also said no to Nazi insanity.

Barth was born in Basel, Switzerland. His father was a Reformed pastor as well as a university professor of New Testament and church history. Barth studied at Europe's finest universities and absorbed the standard liberal line from the top theologians of the day. He spent the first decade of his career pastoring a village church (1911–1921). As he studied the Bible for weekly sermons, and as he witnessed the horrors of World War I, he concluded that liberal theology wasn't scriptural and wasn't true. How could it boast of humanity's essential goodness as thousands were machine-gunned along the trenches of France? Like a child saying the emperor had no clothes, Barth announced that liberalism was bankrupt.

During his academic career at several universities, he watched in horror as the Nazis rose to power. The only thing he found worse than Nazism was the church's accomodation of it. Some in the German church tried to find common ground between Nazism and Christianity, preaching an Aryan Jesus as conqueror of Judaism. Barth rightly interpreted this madness as the result of the church's deviation from Scripture. In 1934 he helped found the Confessing Church, which called the German church back to Christianity and courageously rejected Nazi totalitarianism. As a result, Barth was fired from his teaching position at Bonn. He was granted a professorship of theology at Basel, his hometown, where he stayed until his death.

His *Commentary on Romans* argued that people are completely fallen rather than basically good; therefore, God is not found in us but rather is unreachable unless He chooses to reveal Himself. Christianity is God's truth revealed by His initiative, and salvation comes from God's entering human history in Christ, who was crucified for us.

Barth's ideas were compared to a bomb falling on the

theologians' playground. Liberals howled; conservatives applauded. But the latter were alarmed by perceived problems in his understanding of the Bible's inspiration and its role in Christian life. He said the Bible is not God's Word but instead *contains* God's Word. Rather than being God's direct written revelation, it records people's response to God's revelation.

Barth had critics on both sides, but nearly all believed, then and now, that he was the twentieth century's most significant theologian. Originally from the liberal camp, he tried to bring theology back to a biblical base. Even if he himself didn't return all the way, he buried the hopes of classical liberalism.

However one views Karl Barth's theology, we learn a lesson by his life: a willingness to stand for one's convictions when opposed. And the opposition for him came from both his friends in theology and his enemies, the Nazis. May we be willing to take the Bible seriously, even if doing so costs us friends and angers dangerous foes.

C. S. LEWIS (1898–1963)

Atheist Turned Apologist

On November 22, 1963, the eyes of the world were riveted to their television sets. President John F. Kennedy had been assassinated. Few noticed the passing of Clive Staples (Jack) Lewis the same day.

Lewis was born in Belfast, Northern Ireland, into a Protestant family that loved books. He spent his childhood reading piles of them and writing his own stories. When he was nine, his mother died and he withdrew into himself and his beloved books. Lewis was brought up as a Christian but interpreted his mother's death as God rejecting his prayers, and he became an atheist as a teen.

He studied at Malvern College and Oxford, majoring in English and literature. After a tour of duty in World War I, during which he was wounded by an exploding shell, Lewis returned to school. He graduated, and Oxford made him a fellow in English language and literature (1925–1954). He gave thirty years to Oxford; then Cambridge made him professor of Medieval and Renaissance English literature (1954–1963).

Lewis never stopped reading. Among his favorites were George MacDonald and G. K. Chesterton, both Christians who defied his atheism. Two of Lewis's close friends were Christians, one converted from atheism. While on the Oxford faculty, he befriended J. R. R. Tolkien, author of THE LORD OF THE RINGS trilogy. It dawned on Lewis that most of his friends and favorite authors were Christians and that all of them were brilliant. The wheels began to turn, and he couldn't escape the evidence and logic that supported the gospel. After a long internal battle, he became a Christian at age thirty-three, and his creative juices flowed.

Lewis didn't just write; he blended his vast knowledge and vivid imagination with literary skill like few before or since. The results were more than good; they were classics in every field in which he wrote: children's stories, popular apologetics, and scholarly studies. Among his better-known titles are *The Screwtape Letters* (1942) and THE CHRONICLES OF NARNIA (1950–1956). During the darkest days of World War II, the British Broadcasting Corporation asked him to broadcast seven radio talks. They were wildly popular and were later compiled and published as *Mere Christianity* (1952).

Lewis remained single until his late fifties, when he met and married Joy Davidman Gresham, an American and a former atheist of Jewish descent. Just months after the wedding, she was diagnosed with cancer. But she improved, and they enjoyed three relatively healthy and very happy years before she died in 1960. Lewis was crushed by his loss, and the next year his most personal book, *A Grief Observed*, came out under a pseudonym because it was too intimate for him to put his name on.

Lewis published thirty-nine books and hundreds of shorter pieces: poems, essays, pamphlets, short stories, and critical reviews. The impact of Christianity's most popular defender is impossible to calculate because it hasn't peaked yet. At one point, his books sold two million copies a year, and total sales now approach fifty million, with no end in sight. In five hundred more years, President Kennedy will be largely forgotten, but C. S. Lewis will still be read and cherished.

Knowing Where You're Going

It was not only during the old days that martyrs lived and died. More Christians were killed for their faith in the twentieth century than in all previous centuries combined. And they faced death with faith and courage. No account of final events or words exists for most of them, but we do know the last hours and words of John and Betty Stam. As Communist guards led them to their execution site, observers asked where they were going. John replied that he didn't know where the guards were going, then added, "But we're going to heaven."

The church in China grew rapidly after the Boxer Rebellion in 1900. But the 1920s brought political chaos to the country, and Mao Tse-tung's Communist insurgents took advantage of the instability. As his armies gained control of southern China, he ordered foreign missionaries out. Most left and never returned. But the China Inland Mission (CIM) wanted more missionaries for China, and many went despite the danger.

Elizabeth (Betty) Scott was born in Michigan but was taken to China by her missionary parents before she was one year old. She went to grade school in China, then graduated from high school in Massachusetts and from Wilson College in Pennsylvania before going to Moody Bible Institute in Chicago. John Stam moved from New Jersey to attend Moody and prepare to go to China. They met at a CIM prayer meeting.

China was still considered dangerous, but Betty joined her parents there in 1931; John came the next year. They soon married in her parents' home and welcomed baby Helen into the world a year later. Their first assignment was to Anhui Province, where the Communists had killed missionaries two years before. Despite assurances of safety, Communist soldiers attacked them just two weeks after they arrived, placed them under arrest, and held them for ransom.

As they were force-marched to another town, they overheard soldiers discussing how to get rid of their baby. A Chinese farmer pleaded with the soldiers to spare the baby's life. When they asked him if he would trade his life for hers, he agreed. Whether or not he was serious, they were, and they killed him immediately. No offer was made for John and Betty. They were subjected to public abuse by being paraded through the crowded streets in their underwear, on their way to certain execution.

A Chinese Christian doctor begged in vain to spare their lives, for which he was also sentenced to die. John and Betty were then forced to their knees and beheaded. A day later, a Chinese pastor found three-month-old Helen in an abandoned house and smuggled her in a basket to her grandparents one hundred miles across the mountains.

The Stams' time of service was short, but their impact was big. When news of their martyrdom reached home, hundreds of young people volunteered for the mission field, and giving for missions greatly increased.

As American culture grows increasingly anti-Christian, some Christians think they are being persecuted. That hardly seems a fair assessment compared to the experiences of the true martyrs of the faith. Yet the day may come when American Christians will meet real persecution. Will we face it with the same grace and faith that John and Betty Stam did?

God's Word for Everyone

Nothing compares to a Bible in your native tongue, the language you learned at your mother's knee. It comes alive in a fresh way compared to reading and hearing it in a second language. And Bibles in the hands of common people have altered history. Jerome's translation into Latin, Luther's into German, and Wycliffe's into English gave the Word of God to the masses, and their cultures were changed forever.

During the nineteenth century, the spread of the gospel was matched by Bible translation, producing nearly five hundred new translations for people who had never had a Bible before. Most pioneer missionaries were, in fact, translators. In the twentieth century, the science of linguistics gave Bible translation a new dimension. The leader in the field is Wycliffe Bible Translators (WBT), a nondenominational agency that specializes in linguistics and Bible translation.

The idea for WBT was born in 1917 as William Cameron Townsend (1896–1982) was giving out Spanish Bibles in Central America. Most of the two hundred thousand remote Cakchiquel Indians from rural Guatemala didn't know Spanish, and one asked Townsend why his God didn't speak their language if He was so smart. Townsend devoted the next dozen years to learning their language, and in 1929 he finished a Cakchiquel New Testament. The task proved extremely difficult, but he had discovered God's calling on his life.

Townsend founded WBT in 1934 to provide linguistics training for Bible translators. He named it after fourteenth-century Oxford scholar John Wycliffe, who first translated the Bible into English (see essay 35). In the 1930s and 1940s, WBT began work among Indian tribes in Mexico and Peru. They spread to Asia in 1953 and to Africa in 1962. Since then, they have grown into the world's largest missionary agency, with more than five thousand missionaries assisted by jungle pilots and communications experts. They are currently working on several hundred languages, completing about three dozen translations annually.

Wycliffe Bible Translators and its twin agency, the Summer Institute of Linguistics, teach students how to convert spoken sounds into a written language, create an alphabet, decipher grammar, teach literacy, and translate the Bible. Working closely with native speakers, WBT missionaries have translated the Bible into more than 350 languages and the New Testament into almost nine hundred in more than fifty countries. In the process, most of these languages have been put in writing for the first time.

Despite the progress, the remaining need is enormous. During the twentieth century, the population of the world exploded, and the spread of Christianity exceeded that. Only about one-third of the roughly five thousand languages spoken today have a translated Bible.

Bible translation greatly aids the fulfillment of the Great Commission. God's Word translated into one's native language makes an impact from inside the hearer's culture rather than seeming foreign. The age of missions is far from over. The twenty-first century may surpass the nineteenth as the greatest missionary century ever, and WBT will probably be in the forefront of the work. Young people, retirees, and any Christians seeking a place to serve God might consider Bible translation as a worthy challenge to give one's life to.

DIETRICH BONHOEFFER (1906–1945)

Paying the Price of Discipleship

When Jesus said, "Take up [your] cross and follow me" (Matthew 16:24), His hearers couldn't miss the imagery. The cross was the Roman method of execution. Jesus was telling would-be disciples, "If you're going to follow Me, assume the attitude of a condemned criminal and be ready to die." Dietrich Bonhoeffer revealed how well he understood Jesus by saying, "When Christ calls a man, he bids him come and die."

Bonhoeffer was one of eight children born to Berlin's leading psychiatrist. He studied liberal theology under its last master, Adolf von Harnack, but transferred his academic devotion to Karl Barth. He received his doctorate in theology from Berlin University when he was only twenty-one. Bonhoeffer possessed a brilliant mind and a pastor's heart, desiring ministry more than academia. He was ordained in 1930, when many German pastors were choosing to follow Adolf Hitler.

Opposing the Nazis cost Bonhoeffer his job as chaplain and teacher at Berlin University. For two years he pastored a church in London but returned to Germany to found a small, illegal seminary at Finkenwalde. The Nazis shut it down in 1937 and the next year demanded that pastors swear allegiance to them. Bonhoeffer refused and revisited America, trying to decide where he could best serve. Friends begged him to stay, but he was unwilling to while German Christians faced the Nazi nightmare. He returned to Germany but was forbidden to preach or write. Soon thereafter he joined a plot to assassinate Hitler. It failed.

In 1943 Bonhoeffer was arrested and imprisoned for smuggling Jews into Switzerland. Subjected to solitary confinement and brutal interrogation, he considered suicide so that he wouldn't break and consequently betray his friends. He neither broke nor committed suicide, and in time he was allowed what must have seemed like luxuries: books, writing materials, even visitors. He read, wrote, and comforted other inmates and even guards.

By the spring of 1945, Allied forces were racing across Germany. The Nazis knew their time was up, and Hitler didn't want influential prisoners falling into enemy hands. So on April 9, as Russian forces approached the Flossenberg concentration camp, Bonhoeffer and his friends were hanged. He was thirty-nine. The church gained a martyr; the world lost a hero.

Bonhoeffer's theology was formed in the classroom and the prison cell. True Christianity, he said, goes beyond conversion to a life of discipleship, serving one another as Christ did, even when the cost is high. He spoke and wrote of "religionless Christianity," an active faith that relies more on inner spiritual resources than on outer religious institutions, a Christianity that infuses spiritual reality into everyday life. These ideas were recorded in *Letters and Papers from Prison*, *The Cost of Discipleship*, and *Life Together*, which still inspire and influence Christians and non-Christians alike.

Dietrich Bonhoeffer challenged Christians to replace apathy and cheap grace with disciplined commitment. No better example exists than himself. Bonhoeffer followed Christ all the way to the gallows. The innocent son of privilege, one of the world's great theologians, was murdered by the world's worst criminals.

Christianity is truth to learn and a life to live. Our daily lives, not just Sundays, are to be profoundly affected by what we claim to believe. The true Christian counts the cost of discipleship and pays it.

THE DEAD SEA SCROLLS (1947)

Learning from an Ancient Library

Are the ancient documents on which the church is built still trustworthy after centuries of history? Or has the copying process altered their contents? Archeological finds repeatedly confirm their accuracy, and the discovery of the Dead Sea Scrolls ranks among the most important. That name refers to hundreds of Hebrew, Aramaic, and Greek manuscripts found in eleven caves overlooking a ravine near the northwest corner of the Dead Sea. They had been hiding there for nineteen centuries. But why?

A small Jewish sect had retreated into the wilderness and formed a community called Qumran, anticipating a time of great evil before the end of the world. They were probably Essenes, a group known for separatism and asceticism. Their expectation of the world's demise proved wrong, but hard times did come in response to the Jewish revolt against Rome from AD 66 to 70. The Jewish nation was crushed, resulting in the

Jews' dispersion and the Qumran community's destruction. But someone had the foresight to safeguard their library. Before Roman soldiers arrived, Qumran residents stuffed their manuscripts into clay jars and hid them in caves. They then fled or were killed, but their treasure was safe.

Fast-forward nineteen hundred years. The goat of an Arab shepherd boy wandered away from the herd. As the boy searched for it, he threw a rock into a cave to flush it out. But the sound of breaking pottery instead of a bleating goat scared him, and he ran off. He later returned to investigate and found a bunch of old, clay jars full of manuscript fragments. He had no idea that it was an ancient library. The discovery eventually found its way into the hands of experts, who began to study the writings and reassemble the fragments into whole manuscripts. What they found stunned the scholarly world. Among the documents were one hundred copies of Old Testament books dating from 250 BC to AD 50.

Bible commentators learned things from those Old Testament documents that improved their understanding of some scriptural passages. The nonbiblical books give us insight into the beliefs and practices of the Qumran community as well as the broader Jewish religious scene during Jesus' time. The writings also provide better understanding of the social context within which Christianity began. A few scholars even believe that Jesus knew the Essenes and made some comments in response to their teachings.

The most significant result from the discovery comes from comparing our Old Testament to those very early copies. Our Old Testament is based on the Masoretic text from the ninth and tenth centuries AD, nearly a thousand years later than the Dead Sea Scrolls. Textual scholars determined that our Old Testament is remarkably accurate to the ancient record. The few differences that were found improved modern translations.

Archeological discoveries, such as the Dead Sea Scrolls, demonstrate that the Bible we read and study today is reliable. We can trust it as being accurate to what God revealed to the prophets and apostles. As we learn His truth, we can apply His wisdom to our modern lives, knowing it's what God said.

Get Out or Die!

During the twentieth century, totalitarian systems felt threatened by Christianity and tried to eradicate it within their borders. Brutal measures were taken by the Soviet Union and Communist China to crush the church. In China the persecution began in 1949 when Mao Tse-tung's People's Republic of China ordered foreign missionaries to leave.

The Boxer Rebellion in 1900 had slowed but not ended efforts to reach China for Christ. Despite suspicion of Westerners, missionary work in China continued and flourished. By 1910 the United States and Canada had become the largest providers of international missionaries, and China was their largest field, with almost eighteen hundred North American missionaries serving there.

Some Westerners, however, were less concerned with preaching the kingdom of God than with spreading Western ways, and they considered missions work a means to extend that human-centered vision. Most missionaries didn't share that view, but one foreigner

90

SINCE WWII
(1946–PRESENT)

was the same as another in the eyes of much of the world. Therefore some countries interpreted the presence of missionaries as an Anglo-Saxon invasion of their culture.

Among the most hostile were Mao Tse-tung and his Communist forces. During the 1920s and 1930s, they grew in power and gained territory, especially across southern China. The threat to missionaries was grave. In 1927 alone, half the missionaries in China left for good. Even the most committed fled to safer areas. Many who wouldn't leave the country were executed.

When Mao's Red Army finally overcame Chiang Kai-shek's nationalist party in 1949, he threw out all foreign missionaries, took over church property, and began a system of brutal oppression designed to remove Christianity from China. He believed China's hardships and backward ways were due to Western imperialism and Christianity. He was wrong.

His decree succeeded only on the surface. He rid China of Christian missionaries but not of Christianity. The church remained, the flowering of spiritual seeds planted generations before. But could the national church survive without help from the church in the West? It could. And after generations of missions work, costing thousands of missionary lives, Communist persecution spread the church further and faster than ever before.

Reports from China, especially during the Cultural Revolution (1966–1976), recounted atrocities committed against many elements of society, particularly the church. But as China has gradually opened in recent years, Christians across the world have marveled at the size and vitality of the church there. Estimates run as high as eighty million Christians, with that number growing at a rate of millions a year.

Even the most powerful regimes can't derail God's plan. He shows again and again that He, not government, is sovereign. And Jesus is repeatedly proved to have been right when He said that He would build His church and that the gates of hell would not overcome it (see Matthew 16:18).

Evangelical Giant

I once heard someone say about a smart guy, "He has a one-hundred-pound brain and there's not a blank space in it." Saying that of Carl F. H. Henry might be an under-statement. In America, the mid-twentieth-century shift in religious power from liberals and fundamentalists to evangelicals was pushed along by many people, but by no one more than Henry.

By the 1940s, many conservative theologians had had enough of fundamentalist anti-intellectualism, iso-lationism, and just plain meanness. So a few leading Christians set a new direction between liberal rejection of historic Christianity and fundamentalist rejection of everything else. They formed the National Association of Evangelicals, founded new seminaries and colleges, established publishing houses, and organized ministries to reach young people. Henry's *The Uneasy Conscience of Modern Fundamentalism* (1947) was their manifesto, calling on Christians to engage all of life with intellect and grace while never compromising biblical truth.

Henry was born in New York City, the first of eight

children of German immigrant parents. Two years after graduating from high school on Long Island, he was working for a major New York paper, and friends there led him to Christ. In 1935 he moved to Chicago to attend Wheaton College, where he received a BA and an MA. Almost simultaneously he was taking bachelor of divinity and doctor of theology degrees from Northern Baptist Theological Seminary. Then, to back it all up, he earned a PhD from Boston University in 1949.

What does a guy with a hundred-pound brain and two earned doctorates do with his life? For starters, join the original faculty at Fuller Seminary and become a charter member of the Evangelical Theological Society. In 1955 Henry accepted Billy Graham's offer to become the first editor of *Christianity Today* magazine. He later founded the Institute for Advanced Christian Studies at Eastern Baptist Theological Seminary, where he taught from 1969 to 1974. He then became an international spokesman for World Vision. He also helped found the Council for Biblical Inerrancy in 1977 to bolster the credibility of the conservative Christian view of Scripture.

Henry wrote far too much to list all his works here, but we must note his six-volume *God, Revelation, and Authority* (1976–1983), which argues for classic theism, the Bible's inerrancy, and our need for supernatural revelation. This monumental work is not bedtime reading or something to take on an airplane, but people do read it. Only six months after the first two volumes were released, they sold out and had to be reprinted. When all six volumes came out, Henry was awarded an honorary doctor of divinity degree by Gordon-Conwell Seminary and received a written commendation from President Jimmy Carter.

Henry influenced thinkers and theologians, pastors and evangelists, publishers and politicians, churches and institutions, and ordinary people across the world. As the leading evangelical spokesman, he shaped the movement more than anyone else. He was a towering presence who provided intellectual bedrock beneath the feet of millions of evangelicals, even though few of them knew it. By the end of his life, he had received innumerable awards, including six honorary doctorates in addition to the two he earned.

If evangelicals want to know who they are, they should look to Carl Henry, who blazed the trail. And while most of us do not have hundred-pound brains with all the spaces filled, we can take a cue from Henry and use our brains to the best of our ability.

The Simple Gospel

On football Saturdays, stadiums are full of screaming fans urging their teams on to victory. In those same stadiums, millions have watched Billy Graham preach the gospel. We can't see inner spiritual results, but based on external signs, he must be the most prolific evangelist in history. No one would have expected such renown after his first sermon at age nineteen. After reluctantly agreeing to give the message one Sunday evening, he raced through all four of his forty-five-minute sermons in just eight minutes.

Graham was born into a pious farm family near Charlotte, North Carolina. As a boy, he didn't care much for church but went because he had no choice. When he was sixteen, he and friends took in a revival held by evangelist Mordecai Ham, hoping to get a laugh, but Graham came to Christ instead. After high school, he enrolled at Bob Jones University but found it too restrictive and transferred to Florida Bible Institute. He later went to Wheaton College in Chicago, where he majored in anthropology.

SINCE WWII
(1946–PRESENT) | **92**

Graham began his career in 1943 as a youth pastor in Chicago before joining Youth for Christ. From 1947 to 1951, he served as president of Northwestern Bible College in Minneapolis while preaching small evangelistic campaigns. During his 1949 Los Angeles crusade, several Hollywood celebrities claimed conversion, and publisher Randolph Hearst told his newspaper to push the story. Cities across the country and around the world soon wanted Graham. He eventually conducted several major campaigns each year, many broadcast on national television. Even Communist bloc countries invited Graham to preach.

Graham founded the Billy Graham Evangelistic Association (BGEA) to produce radio broadcasts, films, and *Decision* magazine. He also wrote a syndicated newspaper column and several books, in addition to starting *Christianity Today* with his friend Carl Henry. Over the years, the BGEA organized and led several international conferences on evangelism, attracting thousands of evangelists from nearly every country on earth.

Graham's simple theology—comprising humanity's sinfulness and need of conversion, along with Christ's death on our behalf—may be part of the reason for his success. His messages are clear, easy-to-grasp invitations to receive God's offer of forgiveness and eternal life.

Graham has preached the gospel in more places and to more people than anyone else in history—more than one hundred million in person and unknown millions over the airwaves. Nearly three million have responded. He has been listed repeatedly among the world's most admired people, but he is not without critics. Liberals decry his lack of social engagement; fundamentalists condemn his association with groups they dislike.

Graham has befriended and advised every president since Eisenhower as well as prime ministers, the British queen, and several popes. In the wake of the Watergate scandal, he has been more cautious about political friendships, but for decades America has turned to him as its religious spokesman for national funerals and presidential inaugurations.

His unwavering passion to preach the gospel is an example of faithfulness for all. In our own small spheres, we can each share the good news of Jesus Christ with our families, friends, and others, and we can all strive to imitate Billy Graham's integrity and humility.

JIM ELLIOT (1927–1956)

Supreme Sacrifice

Jim Elliot's parents read the Bible to their children daily, and by the time he entered Wheaton College in 1945, his life was disciplined by that training. He was also convinced that a simple life, free from excess things, was the best way to live for God. His early training and his view of life would serve him well.

After graduation, Elliot knew that God was leading him to those who had never heard of Christ, specifically the Auca Indians of the Amazon River Valley in Ecuador. When reflecting on his decision not to minister to America's youth, he wrote from Ecuador,

> Those Stateside young people have every opportunity to study, hear, and understand the Word of God in their own language, and these Indians have no opportunity whatsoever. . . . When there is that much ignorance over here and so much knowledge and opportunity over there, I have no question in my mind why God sent me here. Those whimpering Stateside young people . . . having a

Bible, are bored with it—while these never heard of such a thing as writing. (Elisabeth Elliot, *Shadow of the Almighty,* p. 237)

In 1955 Elliot formed Operation Auca with fellow missionaries Nate Saint, Pete Fleming, Roger Youderian, and Ed McCully. Their project would be no easy venture. No outsider had successfully settled in Auca territory because for centuries they had killed intruders, including eight Shell Oil employees just twelve years earlier.

From their tiny plane, the men first sighted an Auca village in September 1955. During the following weeks, the missionaries continued their contact by lowering gifts in a bucket at the end of a rope tied to the plane. The decision was made to land, despite warnings not to trust the natives. The men believed the risk was worth it to reach those Stone Age people for Christ.

On January 3, 1956, they landed on a short beach along the Curaray River. Making repeated flights throughout that first day, the men brought in essentials to set up camp. Three days later they made contact with three Aucas, even giving one a ride in the plane. On January 8, while flying over the village, Nate sighted a group moving toward the missionary camp.

He landed to tell Jim and the others, who prepared for the meeting. But soon thereafter all five were speared to death by the Aucas.

Two years later, two of the men's widows began evangelizing the Aucas. The cost had been high, but God's work had started. Many of the natives determined to know God and serve Christ as Elliot had. Furthermore, in response to the sacrifice of Elliot and his friends, hundreds of young Americans committed themselves to missionary service.

Elliot's passion is found in his words quoted in *Shadow of the Almighty* by his wife, Elisabeth.

- "If God wants it that way, I am ready to die for the salvation of the Aucas" (p. 241).

- "Remember, you are immortal until your work is done" (p. 81).

- "He is no fool who gives what he cannot keep to gain what he cannot lose" (p. 247).

- "I seek not a long life, but a full one, like you, Lord Jesus" (p. 247).

Jim Elliot lived only twenty-nine years, but his influence is eternal. As we evaluate ourselves, let us consider that God values the quality of a life more than its length.

MARTIN LUTHER KING JR. (1929–1968)

"I Have a Dream"

On August 28, 1963, two hundred thousand people marched on the U.S. capital. The final speaker at the event was a thirty-four-year-old black pastor from Atlanta, who told the crowd that he had a dream for his children to live in a nation where they would not be judged "by the color of their skin but by the content of their character." The Civil Rights Movement had begun eight years before, but that speech was the first time many white Americans listened.

Since long before the Civil War, racial tensions had been woven into the fabric of American society, including the churches. But that began to change in 1955 in Montgomery, Alabama, when a black woman named Rosa Parks was arrested for refusing to give her bus seat to a white man. Local pastors organized a boycott of city buses and chose Martin Luther King Jr. to lead them. He accepted the offer but insisted that the boycott be peaceful even if whites resorted to violence.

King was named Michael at birth, but his father, a Baptist pastor like his father before him, changed their names to honor the German Reformer (see essay 40). As a boy, King skipped two grades and passed his entrance exams at fifteen to enter Morehouse College. He received his BA and then prepared for ministry by taking a BD at Crozer Theological Seminary and a PhD from Boston University. King's theology combined Jesus' teaching on love with Gandhi's nonviolent means of addressing social injustice.

He began his career as pastor of the Dexter Avenue Baptist Church in Montgomery but soon joined his father as copastor of Ebenezer Baptist Church in Atlanta. In 1957 King helped organize the Southern Christian Leadership Conference, an umbrella agency for other civil rights groups, and from that base he planned nonviolent marches to call attention to civil rights issues.

Because some of his early advisers had Communist ties, King was a target of FBI scrutiny. And he increased the bureau's alarm by criticizing it for cooperating with segregationists. Amid ongoing racism and anti-Communist fears, King was hated by many, including some blacks who called for a militant response to racism. As one of the most controversial figures of his era, King received death threats and was arrested several times. In April 1968 he visited Memphis to speak on behalf of a sanitation workers' strike. The next day, as he stood on a hotel balcony, he was gunned down by an assassin. He was thirty-nine.

King raised awareness of injustice against blacks when many whites couldn't or wouldn't see it. His efforts led to the passage of the Civil Rights Act (1964) and the Voting Rights Act (1965), which mandated desegregation of public facilities and improvements in housing, education, and job opportunities. In 1964 he was awarded the Nobel Peace Prize, and *Time* magazine named him "Man of the Year," the first black person so honored.

King was the biggest figure in America's civil rights movement, acting as the nation's conscience when some people didn't want one. Starting in 1986, the third Monday of January has been designated a national holiday in honor of his birthday. But his greatest legacy is the widened field of opportunities now available for African Americans and members of other minority groups. Martin Luther King Jr. demonstrated what can be accomplished when people apply the love of Christ to social injustice.

FRANCIS SCHAEFFER (1912–1984)

True Truth

Many young Christians of the 1960s and 1970s shared a similar experience. They addressed theological questions to parents or pastors and heard the reply "Don't ask questions; just believe what we tell you and don't think too much." Some turned away from Christianity; if it didn't offer real answers for real questions, why bother? But God did provide answers, and some of those young people heard them from a little man in the Alps who spoke of "true truth"—unchanging truth that touches all of life.

Francis Schaeffer was the only child of a working-class family in Germantown, Pennsylvania. During high school, he became an agnostic. But he discovered answers to his questions by reading the Bible and, as a result, committed himself to Christ. While earning his BA at Hampton-Sydney College, he met and married Edith Seville, who would share in their ministry and become a popular author in her own right. He then did his graduate work at Westminster Theological Seminary and Faith Theological Seminary.

He pastored in Pennsylvania and St. Louis before his church's mission board sent the Schaeffers to Switzerland in 1948 to investigate the battle with theological liberalism in Europe. They stayed, and their ministry took a turn that would shape the lives of thousands. In 1951 Schaeffer underwent a spiritual crisis. After months of thought and inner examination, he emerged fully convinced of his beliefs but with a greater day-by-day experience of the risen Savior. That mix of intellectual truth and spiritual vitality would become a hallmark of his ministry.

While in Switzerland, the Schaeffers often invited international students to their home to discuss the big issues of life and truth, philosophy and religion, art and culture. Schaeffer gave honest, compassionate responses, and the news spread that you could find answers in an out-of-the-way place in the Alps. As an outgrowth of those small-group chats, the Schaeffers founded L'Abri Fellowship in 1955. In the coming years, thousands of students, scholars, and others found intellectual and spiritual refuge there. They returned to their homes, schools, and workplaces to fertilize those areas of life with what they had learned.

Schaeffer's influence reached America in 1968 with the release of *Escape from Reason* and *The God Who Is*

There. People who couldn't go to L'Abri learned how to think from a Christian worldview by reading his books. He eventually wrote twenty-four books, which have sold millions, and released two film series shown in churches across the denominational spectrum. When Schaeffer was diagnosed with cancer in 1978, he and Edith moved to Rochester, Minnesota, to be near the Mayo Clinic. They ministered from there until he died in 1984.

Schaeffer was a philosopher, theologian, teacher, and writer, but he called himself an evangelist, a missionary to the intellectuals. He introduced serious thinking to thousands of Christians who heard the refreshing news that it is okay to think deeply and well. Largely due to Francis Schaeffer, an army of Christians escaped the anti-intellectual ghetto. Many have become serious scholars who now influence the world through their own work.

In an age when churches create specialized ministries for every conceivable group, are we neglecting thinkers? They will shape the coming generations, but who will shape them? We have the opportunity now to design ministries that will find and train them. If we don't seize this opportunity, we may expect to lose them.

Freaks for Jesus

Imagine being a youth leader who offers a church several hundred young converts. You say, "Just take 'em and teach 'em. They don't know a thing, but they just came to Christ and want to learn the Bible and live for Him." Then imagine being told that the young people are welcome in the church only if they will cut their hair, take a bath, and put on shoes. Scenarios like that were repeated often during the Jesus Movement when some leaders tried to direct their young flocks into established churches.

From the mid-1960s to the early 1970s, Western culture was changed by dissatisfied young people searching for a deeper meaning to life. And embedded within the larger counterculture was a smaller movement called the Jesus Revolution. These energetic followers of Jesus, the great Liberator, were an unlikely mix of hippies and former drug users from the streets and straight kids from the churches. Despite differences among various groups, they shared several beliefs: Jesus is the one way, God's Son who can and does change lives, and He

96 | SINCE WWII (1946–PRESENT)

313

is coming back, maybe soon. Everyone can come to Him, no matter their background or their sin or their appearance. It can all be found in the Bible, which is true from cover to cover.

The Jesus Movement began in a storefront mission in San Francisco's Haight-Ashbury district in 1967, the epicenter of the broader countercultural earthquake. Hippie news traveled fast and far, and Jesus communities soon blossomed everywhere. Seattle had its Jesus People Army; Hollywood's Sunset Strip was home to His Place; and smaller cities were not excluded. Young seekers in Omaha, for instance, went to the Christian Brotherhood and the Soul Concern. Jesus freaks on the road stayed at places with names like the JC Power and Light Company in Boulder, Colorado.

Jesus bumper stickers, coffee shops, and newspapers appeared across America and Europe. Larry Norman and other Christian musicians wrote and sang a blend of rock and gospel. Critics in the churches screamed compromise, but Jesus People were reaching kids whom churches wouldn't even let in the door. Campus Crusade started the Christian World Liberation Front at the University of California at Berkeley to reach campus radicals and later pointed out heresies through its Spiritual Counterfeits Project.

By the mid-1970s, the general culture stabilized as the excess of earlier days subsided. What happened to all those Jesus people? For many, when the emotion faded, the fad was over; that's all it was to them. Some drifted away because they couldn't find a church to accept them. A few remained true to the movement, such as Jesus People USA in Chicago. Some founded or joined extremist groups, such as the Alamo Foundation or the Children of God. Many entered evangelical churches, some becoming the pastors and leaders of today. The impact of the Jesus Movement is seen today in the relaxed worship atmosphere of most churches and the contemporary Christian music industry.

Beneath the faddishness and emotion of those times, a genuine revival took place, but most churches missed it. Are churches today more open to reaching, accepting, and teaching people who don't fit their mold? Do we design new forms of ministry as the culture changes? Are we thinking ahead to what society might become in the next decade? If not, we may be left behind, as were some churches during the Jesus Movement. Our message must never change, but if we have no audience, we've not accomplished the mission.

Touching the Untouchables

The twentieth century witnessed the spread of both wealth and poverty. The middle classes in some countries live better than did kings in the past, while the poorest of the poor live like animals. If Jesus' challenge to serve the poor ever fit, it does in this age of enormous disparity. And few applied His challenge more than did Agnes Gonxha Bojaxhiu, known as Mother Teresa, who gave her life to serve the poor, the sick, and the dying.

Mother Teresa was an Indian citizen of Albanian descent, born in Macedonia. Her father died when she was a child, and without his business, the family fell into poverty. Nevertheless, her mother provided a model of service that Agnes couldn't miss. In the midst of their own need, she cared for an invalid neighbor and welcomed six orphans into her home.

When Agnes was twelve, she sensed God calling her to a life of service, and at eighteen she joined an Irish community of nuns who conducted missions in India. A year later she was sent to Calcutta, where she trained to teach geography to schoolgirls at the Loreto Convent.

On weekends she led them into the streets to minister to the poor. For seventeen years, she carried on this dual ministry, teaching her girls and meeting the needs of the poor.

In 1948 she received permission to work solely among the poorest of the poor, starting with a street school for Calcutta's slum children. Leaving behind the relative safety of the convent, she began to live and work among the untouchables of India. In 1950 she founded the Missionaries of Charity to love and care for those who had no one to serve them, and two years later she opened a home for the dying.

Over the years Mother Teresa spread her work to five continents, serving in obscurity until BBC journalist Malcolm Muggeridge conducted a television interview with her in 1969. After he produced a book and a film on her life and work, Harvard gave her an honorary doctorate. She was recognized by Queen Elizabeth and the U.S. Congress, and received the Nobel Peace Prize in 1979.

None of the praise compromised Mother Teresa's commitment to the poor. Her death from a heart attack at eighty-seven was overshadowed by the death of Britain's Princess Diana, only days before. But from the rich and powerful to the poor and destitute, the world mourned her passing.

Mother Teresa served all and feared none. Her life of sacrifice was matched by her tenacious dealing with government officials and church representatives. Even during her lifetime she was revered by people from every religion and worldview across the globe. More than four thousand nuns now serve in hundreds of homes she founded in many countries to serve the sick, the poor, and the dying.

No matter how lowly the labor or great the cost, Mother Teresa served those who needed it most. She understood and applied Jesus' words "Whatever you did for one of the least of these brothers of mine, you did for me" (Matthew 25:40). Her life is a convicting reminder that churches and individual Christians can minister to the needy by acts of simple kindness. Christians can still bear the load and reap the joy of serving the suffering.

ALEXANDER SOLZHENITSYN (1918–)

One Person Can Change the World

Soviet dissident Alexander Solzhenitsyn was born one year after the Bolshevik Revolution of 1917. Raised Russian Orthodox, he was converted to Marxism-Leninism by the Soviet education system. He took his degree in science but loved literature and dreamed of fame from writing the glories of Russia's revolution.

In 1941 the Red Army drafted him to fight the Nazis, and by 1945 he had risen to the rank of captain. He once referred to Stalin as "the mustachioed one" in a private letter—a big mistake. During "Uncle Joe's" reign of terror, people were arrested for anything, and the secret police got their hands on that letter. Captain Solzhenitsyn would pay for his indiscretion with eight years of his life.

In the federal prison system, called the Gulag, he was exposed to the worst and best of humanity, including believers whose faith under hellish conditions challenged his atheism. Anatoly Silin made a deep impression. A teacher of literature with no religious training, Silin wrote and memorized theologically rich poetry in his head and shared it with anyone willing to listen, including Solzhenitsyn. There in prison Solzhenitsyn came to Christ, and he too began to write in his head. Someday, if released, he would tell the world the truth about the Soviet Union.

Had the Soviets been wiser, they would not have released Solzhenitsyn. But they did in 1953, and he revealed the Gulag's unspeakable brutality. He earned worldwide acclaim for *One Day in the Life of Ivan Denisovich*, depicting a typical day in the Gulag based on his own experience. The world was aghast, and Solzhenitsyn became a hero. In his other works he reported how the revolution had led to sixty million deaths.

To the Kremlin's embarrassment, Solzhenitsyn was awarded the Nobel Prize for literature in 1970. He backed it up with his massive *Gulag Archipelago*, further exposing the horrors of Soviet concentration camps. Before this time, only staunch anti-Communists believed the rumors from behind the walls. But now the whole world knew that the workers' paradise was one big prison, maintained by terror and murder. That proved too much for Soviet leaders, and in 1974 they exiled Solzhenitsyn to the West. Most of his books had to be smuggled out of the Soviet Union to be published, and now he himself was kicked out—too much trouble to keep, too famous to kill.

The West was ecstatic with the Cold War victory. But the fiery prophet turned out not to be the champion of modern Western values as expected. After taking on the evil empire, why would he fear the wimpy West? In 1978 he tongue-lashed elites at Harvard for abandoning their Christian heritage, which had set their moral compass for centuries. The West, he said, had not lost God to tyranny but had abandoned Him for materialism and decadence. Many who had praised Solzhenitsyn now vilified him.

Nevertheless, Alexander Solzhenitsyn has been called the dominant writer of our age, whose work ushered in the demise of the world's last empire. From the Gulag to Harvard, he proved how unpopular the truth can be. But God honors truth and uses one person of truth to change the world. As followers of the Truth, we are to speak whatever the setting or the cost.

And the Wall Came Tumbling Down

One of today's hot issues is the so-called separation of church and state. But that idea is something of a joke. Every state affects the church, often for the worse, as seen in the former Soviet Union.

After Russia fell to Communism in 1917, Vladimir Lenin attacked the church. He died in 1924, but his successor, Joseph Stalin, picked up the pace, hitting his stride during the purges of the late 1930s. Millions of Russians, many of them Christians, were wiped out like bugs. Hitler gets press for killing six million, but Stalin holds the record: about sixty million.

The Russian Orthodox Church, even though deeply embedded in the culture and soul of Russia through a thousand years of history, was devastated. Survivors were sometimes forced to work as the religious wing of the KGB, the Soviet Union's secret police. Evangelicals, who had been in Russia for only a century, were targeted for extermination. World War II deflected Stalin's attention for a while, but when it ended, the reign of terror resumed. As the decades rolled on, Department 5 of the KGB continued to pursue, imprison, torture, and kill Christians. Nevertheless, despite unimaginable atrocities, the church clung to life under this totalitarian regime.

In the mid-1980s Mikhail Gorbachev came to power, promoting ideas of openness and cooperation. In a few years, massive protests in Eastern Europe, led in part by Christians, shook the Soviet world. In 1989 Soviet satellite states in Eastern Europe saw their chance to escape the chains they had worn since World War II. One after the other, countries ran through the crack in the door that Gorbachev had opened, and the Berlin Wall—symbolic of the Iron Curtain—was torn down. Finally, in 1990 under President Boris Yeltsin, Russia announced its independence from the Union of Soviet Socialist Republics. Most of the republics were already independent of that union, so it no longer existed except as a name. It formally disbanded in 1991.

At last Christians in Russia could gather openly to worship and to preach the Bible. Millions of unbelievers wanted to taste the forbidden fruit of Christianity. Western Christians flooded Russia, Ukraine, and other republics and reported stunning numbers of converts.

But many of those evangelistic efforts bypassed the existing churches, which had suffered so much, sometimes straining relations between Western and Eastern believers. And, it turns out, many of the converts were responding more out of curiosity than out of conviction.

Today the church in the former Soviet Union sometimes faces opposition from local or regional officials, especially where Islam is strong. In other places, Christians have free rein to operate as they wish. Differences between Orthodox and evangelical churches run deep, but the big story is that God's people survived; the Soviet thugs did not.

As Christians living in freedom, do we take for granted what we have? Governments that are hostile to Christianity may use ruthless means to exterminate the church. They will fail in the end, but that's no excuse for relaxing our vigilance to preserve liberty now. If we are wise, we will use our freedom well, for we may not have it forever.

Into the Future

The vitality and leadership of the church has traveled westward from Judea to Europe to North America and now to Asia. It has also jumped the equator from North to South, into Africa and Latin America. The number of Christians in the Third World has boomed in the last generation, and they are sending missionaries to the rest of the world. God is raising them up as the Western church seems increasingly swamped by its own culture.

One reason for the slippage of the Western church is its failure to heed the warnings of the last century. We already noted one from J. Gresham Machen: False ideas are the greatest obstacle to the reception of the gospel (see essay 83). But he was not the only voice. Speaking at the opening of the Billy Graham Center at Wheaton College in 1980, Lebanese statesman Charles Malik warned that our greatest danger is anti-intellectualism in the church; we are abandoning the arena of debate to our foes. American believers seem unaware or unconcerned that an intellectual war is

100 | SINCE WWII (1946–PRESENT)

being waged on Christianity. And it strikes deeper than politics; it goes to the core of thinking about all of life from a Christian worldview. If we are to recapture some influence, all Christians (not just the professionals: our scholars, pastors, teachers, and writers) must become intellectually engaged.

Ironically, as America's Christian masses spurn the life of the mind, our scholars are among the world's elite. And a few visionary believers have had the foresight to establish Christian think tanks to penetrate the broader culture with a Christian worldview. These ministries are often strategically located near universities, the trend-setters and trainers of future generations.

God has also given the American church two resources that the rest of the church desperately needs: money and teachers. And He's using the first to send the second around the world to train nationals. He does this through schools like Donetsk Christian University in Ukraine, which trains and sends pastors and Christian workers across the former Soviet Union. And He uses high-tech ministries like the Internet Biblical Seminary to teach leaders in places where poverty prevents them from attending school or where it's illegal to receive Christian training.

The current wave of Christian growth is most visible

in China. When the Communists expelled Western missionaries in 1949, after a century of work, only a tiny fraction of the people were Christians. Over the next thirty years, government oppression hindered but did not prevent church growth, and when Beijing slightly relaxed its policy on religion in the mid-1980s, the church spread with stunning speed. Despite persecution, that trend continues. Estimates of Christians in China are notoriously hard to make, but they now range from twenty to eighty million. Whatever the number, the significant factor is that the growth resulted almost entirely from national efforts, not Western.

Every Christian must decide how God would use him or her in His eternal plan. For most American believers, the starting point is bluntly obvious: Will I pursue the ideals of Western culture (usually centered on me, my feelings, and my stuff) or will I sacrifice everything to have an impact for eternity?

After twenty centuries of church history, you and I are now playing our part, which will be recorded in heaven for all to read. As we live our faith day by day, following in the footsteps of our spiritual ancestors, each of us should ask, *When it comes time to die, what difference will it make that I have lived?*

Index of People, Movements, and Events

APPENDIX B

Recommended Resources

Bingham, D. Jeffrey. *Pocket History of the Church.* Downers Grove, IL: InterVarsity, 2002.

Brauer, Jerald C., and others, eds. *The Westminster Dictionary of Church History.* Philadelphia: Westminster, 1971.

Cahill, Thomas. *How the Irish Saved Civilization: The Untold Story of Ireland's Heroic Role from the Fall of Rome to the Rise of Medieval Europe.* New York: Doubleday, 1995.

Cairns, Earle Edwin. *Christianity Through the Centuries,* 10th ed. Grand Rapids, MI: Zondervan, 1969.

Dowley, Tim, et al., ed. *Eerdmans Handbook to the History of Christianity.* Grand Rapids, MI: Eerdmans, 1977.

Edwards, Jonathan, ed. *The Life and Diary of David Brainerd.* Grand Rapids, MI: Baker, 1989.

Elliot, Elisabeth. *Shadow of the Almighty: The Life and Times of Jim Elliot.* San Francisco: Harper & Row, 1958.

Elwell, Walter A., ed. *Handbook of Evangelical Theologians.* Grand Rapids, MI: Baker, 1993.

Hill, Jonathan. *The History of Christian Thought.* Downers Grove, IL: InterVarsity, 2003.

Kreeft, Peter. *Christianity for Modern Pagans: Pascal's Pensées Edited, Outlined, and Explained.* San Francisco: Ignatius, 1993.

Magill, Frank N., and Ian P. McGreal, eds. *Christian Spirituality: The Essential Guide to the Most Influential Spiritual Writings of the Christian Tradition.* San Francisco: Harper & Row, 1988.

Marsden, George M. *Fundamentalism and American Culture: The Shaping of Twentieth-Century Evangelicalism, 1870–1925.* New York: Oxford University Press, 1980.

McKim, Donald K., ed. *Historical Handbook of Major Biblical Interpreters.* Downers Grove, IL: InterVarsity, 1998.

Noll, Mark A. *America's God: From Jonathan Edwards to Abraham Lincoln.* Oxford: Oxford University Press, 2002.

———. *Turning Points: Decisive Moments in the History of Christianity.* Grand Rapids, MI: Baker, 1997.

Noll, Mark A., and others, eds. *Eerdmans Handbook to Christianity in America.* Grand Rapids, MI: Eerdmans, 1983.

Olson, Roger E. *The Story of Christian Theology: Twenty Centuries of Tradition and Reform.* Downers Grove, IL: InterVarsity, 1999.

Piper, John. *A Godward Life: Savoring the Supremacy of God in All of Life.* 2 vols. Sisters, OR: Multnomah, 1997, 1999.

Reid, Daniel G., et al., eds. *Dictionary of Christianity in America.* Downers Grove, IL: InterVarsity, 1990.

Sala, Harold J. *Heroes: People Who Made a Difference in Our World.* Urichsville, OH: Promise Press, 1998.

Shelley, Bruce L., *Church History in Plain Language.* Waco, TX: Word, 1982.

Shelley, Bruce L., comp. *All the Saints Adore Thee: Insight from Christian Classics.* Grand Rapids, MI: Zondervan, 1988.

Tucker, Ruth A. *From Jerusalem to Irian Jaya: A Biographical History of Christian Missions.* Grand Rapids, MI: Zondervan, 1983.

Wakefield, Gordon S., ed. *The Westminster Dictionary of Christian Spirituality.* Philadelphia: Westminster, 1983.

Wegner, Paul D. *The Journey from Texts to Translations: The Origin and Development of the Bible.* Grand Rapids, MI: Baker, 1999.

In addition to these books, *Christian History* magazine is also a valuable resource for those interested in the history of the church. See online at <www.christianitytoday.com/history/>.

Author

Dr. Rick Cornish previously taught theology for seven years in the former Soviet Union. A graduate of Denver Seminary, Rick lives in Minnesota with his wife, Tracy. They have two sons, Scott and Ben (the original and most important audience for this book), who are both in college.